Dior

BY DIOR

Dior

BY DIOR

THE AUTOBIOGRAPHY OF CHRISTIAN DIOR

Translated by Antonia Fraser

V&A Publishing

First published by Weidenfeld & Nicolson, 1957
This edition published by V&A Publishing, 2018
V&A Publishing
Victoria and Albert Museum
South Kensington
London SW7 2RL
vam.ac.uk/publishing

Distributed in North America by Abrams,
an imprint of ABRAMS

E-book edition
ISBN 978 1 85177 671 9

Paperback edition
ISBN 978 1 85177 978 9

10 9 8 7 6 5
2024 2023 2022 2021

A catalogue record for this book is available from
the British Library.

Cover illustration © Beatriz Lostalé 2018

Printed and bound by CPI Group (UK) Ltd, Croydon

V&A Publishing

Supporting the world's leading
museum of art and design,
the Victoria and Albert
Museum, London

CONTENTS

PROLOGUE

THE TWO CHRISTIAN DIORS

Reviewers often describe authors of memoirs as 'leaning on their past'. I have never liked this expression: for one thing it suggests that the writer needs to 'lean' on something, and for another, it implies that his past is already dead and done with. I should like to say straight away that I feel no need to 'lean' on my past for support, and I certainly feel no false nostalgia for it. I am convinced that my finest memories are yet to come, and that even my past lies only just behind me.

After all, Christian Dior is only nine years old – which explains why the most interesting thing about him, for me, is not what has happened to him in the past, but what is going to happen to him in the future.

You will gather from this that there are two Christian Diors: and I am speaking now of Christian Dior, *couturier*, of Maison Christian Dior, 30 avenue Montaigne, born 1947. It was in order to tell the truth about this second nine-year-old Christian Dior that the first Christian Dior decided to write this book. He had been the subject of quite enough inaccurate discussion already, and I felt it was time to let the world know the real facts about him.

In any case, I was afraid that if I waited any longer, I might find that I myself had grown too far away from my subject. Personally, I always find the early years, when a man is carving out his career, the most exciting part of any autobiography. Unfortunately, once he has left these years behind and entered a more secure phase, all too often he can no longer understand and recreate the aspirations of the man he once was.

Alas, the writing of this book has involved me in a completely alien form of expression. I undertook it with many misgivings, and survey the results without the slightest conceit. Conceit! Some of my readers will smile when they see this and think that since I have written a book entirely centred on myself, my career, and my profession, it is rather strange for me to deny that I am conceited. Let me make myself clear. In this book I shall only discuss subjects about which I know, and can therefore speak with authority. I assume that those who are not interested in *haute couture* and its ramifications, will not be interested in reading my book either: whereas those who are will assuredly understand and sympathize with my reasons for wanting to write it. I have not touched on subjects about which I have no expert knowledge – such as abstract art or the reform of the constitution. To my mind, that would be real conceit.

I am a good deal less confident about my handling of the problem of the two Christian Diors – Christian Dior the public figure, and Christian Dior the private individual. The former, whom you will principally read about in this book, is the famous *couturier*. Ensconced in a magnificent house in the avenue Montaigne, he is a compound of people, dresses, stockings, perfumes, publicity handouts, press photographs, and every now and then, a small bloodless (but inky!) revolution whose reverberations are felt all over the world.

Perhaps I should have concentrated entirely on him, and let nothing of myself peep through. For I present a very different sort of picture: I was born at Granville in Normandy on January 21, 1905, the son of Alexandre Louis Maurice Dior, manufacturer, and Madeleine Martin, his wife. I am half Parisian, therefore, and half Norman, and I am still very attached to my native Normandy, although I rarely go there now. I like all the simple things of life, such as small parties of old friends; I detest the noise and bustle of the world, and sudden, violent changes.

Yet to suppress this shrinking character altogether would have seemed to me a form of cheating; it would also have deprived my story of some of its personal touches.

My celebrated fellow countryman, Gustave Flaubert, once defended one of the characters in his novels to a court with the bold words: 'I *am* Madame Bovary'. And were that other Christian Dior ever to involve me in a similar situation, I should certainly defend him with my last breath: 'I *am* he'. For whether I like the thought or not, my inmost hopes and dreams are expressed in *his* creations.

PART ONE

THE BIRTH OF MAISON CHRISTIAN DIOR

— 1 —

THE RELUCTANT COUTURIER

The most important feature of my life – I would be both ungrateful and untruthful if I failed to acknowledge it immediately – has been my good luck; and I must also acknowledge my debt to the fortune-tellers who have predicted it.

I first had my fortune told when I was very young. It was in 1919, at a bazaar near my home, organized to raise funds for the soldiers. There was every kind of sideshow and we all took some part in it. I dressed myself up as a gypsy, suspended a basket round my neck by ribbons, and sold lucky charms. In the evening, when the crowds were thinning out, I found myself next to the fortune-teller's booth. She offered to read my palm.

'You will suffer poverty,' she said. 'But women are lucky for you, and through them you will achieve success. You will make a great deal of money out of them, and you will have to travel widely.'

At the time I attached absolutely no importance to her prediction, which seemed to me to be complete nonsense, but when I went home I reported it faithfully to my parents. The ambiguous phrase: 'You will make a great deal of money out of women' has since been fully explained, but at the time it must have seemed as strange to my parents as it did to me – they were certainly as ignorant of the white slave trade as they were of *haute couture*! And they would as soon have believed that their son could be involved in one as in the other. The threat of poverty also seemed inexplicable, and as for travel – there were roars of laughter in the family circle:

'Imagine Christian a great traveller! Think of the fuss he makes just going to see a friend.'

I wonder if my parents would have recognized me at the end of 1945 when the adventure of Christian Dior was just beginning? I scarcely recognized myself. I had spent ten happy years in the world of *haute couture*, as a designer at Lucien Lelong; it was a delightful existence – I had none of the responsibilities of putting my designs into practice, on the one hand, nor the burden of an executive job on the other. With the end of the war, the departure of the army of occupation, and above all the return home of my sister who had been deported (a return incidentally which had been obstinately predicted by a fortune-teller, even at the worst moments of our despair), I was free once more to lead the life of peaceful anonymity which I loved. An unhappy chapter of my life had ended. On the fresh, still unblemished page before me, I hoped to record nothing but happiness.

My optimism enabled me to forget temporarily that we were still living in the aftermath of a terrible war. Traces of it were all around me – damaged buildings, devastated countryside, rationing, the black market, and less serious, but of more immediate interest to me, hideous fashions. Hats were far too large, skirts far too short, jackets far too long, shoes far too heavy ... and worst of all, there was that dreadful mop of hair raised high above the forehead in front, and rippling down the backs of the French women on their bicycles.

I have no doubt that this *zazou* style originated in a desire to defy the forces of occupation and the austerity of Vichy. For lack of other materials, feathers and veils, promoted to the dignity of flags, floated through Paris like revolutionary banners. But as a fashion I found it repellent.

There was only one wartime custom which I was sad to see disappearing: lack of petrol had forced us all to go everywhere on foot and, without realizing it, we Parisians had begun to enjoy these pleasant strolls which led to chance encounters with our friends and long idle gossips *en route*.

It was in fact in the course of one of these pilgrimages from the rue Saint Florentin to the rue Royale, where I was then living, that I actually met my fate! It appeared to me in the rather humdrum shape of a childhood friend, with whom I had played long ago on the beach at Granville, and whom I had not seen for years. He was now a director of Gaston, a *couture* house in the rue Saint Florentin, and had apparently heard that I had become a designer.

Gesturing wildly, he exclaimed that our meeting was the most wonderful coincidence. Marcel Boussac, the owner of Gaston, wanted to reorganize the whole house drastically and was busy looking for a designer capable of infusing new life into it. Did I know the man-in-a-million capable of undertaking this formidable task? I thought hard for a few moments before telling him regretfully that I could think of no one who would do ... I still wonder why I never thought of suggesting myself.

However, Fate did not let me escape so easily. I ran into my old friend of the beach a second time, on exactly the same pavement between the rue Saint Florentin and the rue Royale. He still had not found his man-in-a-million. It still did not occur to me to suggest myself.

Before making a third attempt, Fate prepared the scene a little. Pierre Balmain, one of my fellow designers at Lelong, decided to leave and start a new house under his own name – very successfully, as it has turned out. This had the effect of making me think seriously about my own future; for the first time, I wondered whether I was really devoid of personal ambition. It was true that I was extremely happy at Lelong and got on well with everyone there, but I was working all the time to achieve the financial success of another man. I was also toiling in the bonds of his creative inspiration, since my loyalty to Lelong prevented me from expressing my own rather different ideas.

When Fate brought me face to face with the inquiring face of my friend for the third time, on the same piece of pavement, my mind was made up. Without realizing for a moment that I was altering the whole course of my life, I said boldly:

'After all this, would I do?'

These comparatively harmless words were scarcely out of my mouth than I was overcome with horror. I suddenly foresaw the dreadful consequences of my rashness. First of all, I should have to meet the famous Marcel Boussac, head of the *Comptoir de l'Industrie Cotonnière* (CIC), which alone seemed an insurmountable obstacle to someone as shy as me. But that was not all. I should have to deal with a host of business men who knew nothing about *couture*, and the very word 'business', with its sinister implications, had always terrified me. Worst of all was the prospect of something called a 'business lunch'. Hitherto I had always associated lunch with the infinitely pleasanter topic of food! Now, before meeting Marcel Boussac for the first time, I was to talk things over with his right-hand man, M. Fayol, in the course of one of these grim functions.

I was greatly relieved to find that M. Fayol wore neither a black jacket, nor striped trousers, nor a stiff collar; the pockets of his waistcoat were not stuffed with agenda, memoranda, and fountain pens, and, like me, he enjoyed his food. Best of all, he did not cross-examine me with searching questions and try to trip me up when I answered. A large, kindly, good-natured man, he was anxious to put me at my ease, and was completely straightforward in his discussions with me. Furthermore he appreciated feminine elegance, because his own wife, Nadine Picard, adored clothes. At all events, he seemed prepared to believe that my ignorance of business was not a sign of mental deficiency and, for my part, I hope I didn't create the impression of a guileless innocent trying to earn his living in a hard world!

As a matter of fact, that was exactly how I thought of myself, and it took me a long time to overcome this complex of mine. Having entered very late into this profession where others had spent a lifetime learning, and having had no training to guide me except my own instincts, I had always been afraid of betraying my ignorance of it. Perhaps it was this very fear of remaining the perpetual amateur that spurred me on to brush aside my doubts at last, and invent the character of Christian Dior, *couturier*.

When M. Fayol and I parted, I think we were quite pleased with what we had seen of each other. We agreed that the first essential step was for me to pay an extended visit to Maison Gaston, in order to see how the business was run. It was a splendid excuse for me to put off making any serious decision and delay the fatal day when I would have to leave Lelong.

Three days later I entered what had first been christened with a great flourish, in the summer of 1925, 'Maison Philippe et Gaston'. As a schoolboy, I remembered gazing at the exquisite pastel-coloured clothes which the beautiful Hughette Duflos had bought from this house. Later it became quite simply 'Gaston', and unfortunately suffered a great deal from wartime difficulties and restrictions; it now only dealt with furs, and had an old-fashioned atmosphere which, personally, I thought it would be impossible to get rid of.

I inspected the whole business from top to bottom most conscientiously, but from the word go I was convinced that Marcel Boussac would be wasting his time and money in trying to restore Gaston to its former glory. So many others before me had tried to resurrect once famous names without success: the existence of a *couture* house is fraught with dangers and its life-span is often far shorter than that of the men who run it. My heart sank at the thought of the hazards involved; the cobwebs which would have to be swept away, the difficulties of coping with a staff which had been set in its ways for so many years and would certainly resent changes – in short, the impossibility of making 'something new out of something old' in a trade where novelty is all important. As I left Gaston, I decided that I was not meant by nature to raise corpses from the dead.

The answer was definitely no.

I must admit that I was secretly very relieved. Now I would not have to face Lelong with the news that I was leaving: I would not have to take an interest in 'business'; I could sink back into my pleasant little rut, to which I was so sentimentally attached. After so many years of hardship I was prepared to cling tenaciously to it.

Consequently I went to CIC the next morning with a light heart, knowing that nothing would come of it, because I intended to refuse Boussac's offer politely but firmly. I found him waiting for me and took an instantaneous liking to both the man and his surroundings. There were plenty of books, some beautiful pieces of Empire furniture and a desk on which a bronze racehorse (a model of one of the favourites of the master of the house) had pride of place. Behind it, on the wall, hung a *gouache* of Rome.

In the centre of all this was the great man himself. Of medium height and stockily built, he had a determined forehead, square jaw, and very precise speech and gestures; but a genuinely charming smile lit up this otherwise rather severe appearance. As I sat down facing him, I suddenly realized what my true ambition was. Here was a famous financier, who was at the same time a man of wide and cultivated intelligence. I knew him already to be the son of Mme Jeanne Catulle-Mendès and the husband of Fanny Heldy, whom I had so often admired at the opera. Obviously his interests extended far wider than the two subjects on which I was so lamentably ignorant – money and horses. I felt that we should get on extremely well together.

Shy people often have a very abrupt way of speaking. I suddenly heard myself telling him that what I really wanted to do was not to resurrect Gaston, but create a new *couture* house under my own name, in a district of my own choosing. I wanted a house in which every single thing would be new: from the *ambiance* and the staff, down to the furniture and even the address. All around us, life was beginning anew: it was time for a new trend in fashion. Greatly daring, I described the house of my dreams. It would be small and secluded, with very few workrooms; within them the work would be done according to the highest traditions of *haute couture*; the clothes, which would give an impression of simplicity, would in fact involve elaborate workmanship and would be aimed at a *clientèle* of really elegant women. After the long war years of stagnation, I believed that there was a genuine unsatisfied desire abroad for something new in fashion. In order to meet this demand, French *couture* would have to return to the traditions of great luxury: which was why I envisaged my house as a craftsman's workshop, rather than a clothes factory.

Out of breath, and amazed at my own temerity, I stopped short. Marcel Boussac had heard me out with great patience and, before escorting me to the door, he told me that although I had outlined quite a different plan to him from the one he had envisaged, and mine was perhaps rather over-ambitious, nevertheless my ideas interested him and he would like to have time to think them over. Secretly I felt that he must have been amazed at my own high opinion of myself! As for me, I was still suffering from the shock of discovering that having gone to see him in order to say 'no', I ended up by outlining a plan which sounded very like 'yes'.

Several days elapsed before I heard that the Boussac group were definitely interested in my project – days in which I suffered tortures of doubt. I had begun to hope so fervently that nothing would come of it that this favourable reply horrified me. Was I going to have to break the news of my departure to Lucien Lelong – who also happened to be a great personal friend of Marcel Boussac – after all? What on earth had I let myself in for?

But I had gone too far to turn back now. I could no longer conceal from myself that I had entered into definite negotiations with the Boussac group. However, as we began to plan the details of the business, unexpected difficulties arose. On my side, my intransigence arose not from conceit, but from a secret unacknowledged desire to escape from the whole thing. This feeling of panic eventually led me to send a telegram breaking off negotiations completely.

It was at this juncture that I went to see Madame Delahaye, the fortune-teller who had obstinately predicted that my sister would return from deportation.

She ordered me sternly to accept the Boussac offer at once. 'You *must* create the house of Christian Dior, whatever the conditions,' she told me. 'Nothing anyone will offer you later will compare with the chance which is open to you now.'

In face of her complete confidence in my future, I bowed my head, or to be honest, I resigned myself to the inevitable. A telephone call to M. Fayol and a few hasty explanations undid the effects of my telegram of refusal. Negotiations were resumed. My fit of bad temper had been exhausted and it now proved unexpectedly easy to reach an agreement with M. Boussac.

I plucked up my courage to break the news of my departure to Lelong, or rather I went and discussed it first with Madame

Raymonde. It was she who had introduced me to Lelong: we had become great friends, and in the past she had frequently given me excellent advice, acting as my guardian angel. I had hinted to her some time back about my negotiations with the Boussac group, and she had made up her own mind to leave the avenue Matignon with me, in order to back me up in my new enterprise. It was more for my sake than for hers, that she asked a friend to go and consult another very secret fortune-teller called the Grandmother about the future of my house.

Apparently when she was shown a piece of paper on which I had scribbled a few meaningless sentences, the Grandmother went into raptures:

'This is astonishing!' she exclaimed. 'This house is going to revolutionize fashion!'

She painted such a dazzling picture of the future that we did not dare to believe all she told us. But the mere fact that her verdict agreed with that of my own fortune-teller gave me the necessary impetus to break the news to Lelong. In spite of all his promises, above all in spite of my deep personal attachment to him, I stuck to my guns that I was leaving, with Mme Raymonde and Mme Delahaye to back me up. It was decided that I should do two more collections for Lelong, in order to be able to show round my successor.

I can never thank Lelong sufficiently for the kindness and understanding which he showed me in accepting the fact that my mind was made up. We parted on the best of terms – in fact the only flaw in our parting was my own regret at leaving a house where I had been so peacefully happy for so long.

Once I had quitted my dear friend and most generous employer, the worry of finding a suitable house in which to set up my new business became uppermost in my mind. I knew exactly what I wanted – it was the house which I had described to Marcel Boussac – but I had no idea where to find it. Many years before my decisive interview with him, I had in fact stopped short in front of two small houses side by side in the avenue Montaigne – numbers 28 and 30. To my friend Pierre Colle, the art dealer, who was with me, I pointed out their neat, compact proportions, and air of sober elegance without the least hint of ostentation. Pierre had been the first person to suggest that he should put up the money for a *couture* house in my name and, as we stood in front of the twin facades, I said to him jokingly:

'Pierre, if your idea ever comes off, I am determined to set myself up here and nowhere else!'

But in 1945 there was absolutely no reason for thinking that either of these two houses was for sale. My first move was to turn to the agencies, who supplied me with a number of addresses, all in the same part of the Champs-Élysées. The houses they suggested were all extremely smart: the first, in the place François 1er, has since been bought by Madame Manguin. The other, in the avenue Matignon, was enormous, and is now the property of my great friend and fellow *couturier*; Jean Dessès. I could not bring myself to decide in favour of either of these houses. Neither of them was on the modest scale which I had pictured to Marcel Boussac, neither of them was quite *my* sort of house. At the same time, I could not put off making a decision much longer.

So there I was – distracted by my own indecision, which might prove fatal to my whole enterprise, but unable to put an end to it.

It was at this point that somebody remarked quite casually:

'If you're looking for a house in this area, why don't you try the avenue Montaigne. The dress shop at No. 30 is closing down.'

Sure enough, I discovered that the lease was for sale. And Maison Christian Dior was born.

— 2 —

A HOUSE OF ONE'S OWN

In my case, 'being my own master', far from meaning that I was free to do as I pleased, meant that I was faced with the urgent problem of making a success of my new venture. I was now responsible for the entire organization of the future Maison Christian Dior, although I willingly left the details of the administration to the Boussac group which had backed it financially.

But neither administrative efficiency nor financial backing could ensure success, which depended entirely on my creative flair, if any. I knew that if I were to emerge victorious in this war of the knife (or the scissors!) I had to be equipped with a first-class *état-major*, or general staff. I already had Raymonde, whose vigilance and sensitivity to every passing trend of fashion were belied by her serene appearance. Raymonde was to become my second self – or to be more accurate, my other half. She is my exact complement: she plays Reason to my Fantasy, Order to my Imagination, Discipline to my Freedom, Foresight to my Recklessness, and she knows how to introduce peace into an atmosphere of strife. In short, she has supplied me with all those qualities which I have never had time to acquire for myself, and has steered me successfully through the intricate world of fashion, in which I was still a novice in I947. It is difficult to define Mme Raymonde's exact position in my house: let it suffice to say that she holds the reins of the business in her firm and capable grasp, and applies her invaluable good sense and warm humanity to everything she does.

Having acquired Mme Raymonde, I next turned to Mme Bricard, who had helped Molyneux with his collections to great effect. We had become great friends: Mme Bricard is one of those people, increasingly rare, who make elegance their sole *raison d'être*. Gazing at life out of the windows of the Ritz, so to speak, she is superbly indifferent to such mundane considerations as politics, finance, or social change. In August she allows herself to spend a month at a fashionable watering-place in order that she may be seen in the square or the casino, but on the whole her love of the country and nature does not go further than the flowers with which she decorates her hats and her dresses. Her high standards are inflexible: in fashion she aims immediately for the most marked expression of that indefinable, and perhaps slightly neglected thing called *chic*.

Mme Bricard is completely cosmopolitan in her elegance, and I felt that her remarkable character, her inimitable extravagances of taste, would have an excellent effect on the phlegmatic temperament which I had inherited from my Norman forebears. I knew that her presence in my house would inspire me towards creation, as much by her reactions – and even her revolts – *against* my ideas, as by her agreements. Her deep knowledge of the traditions of *haute couture* and her refusal to compromise seemed the best possible stimulants for a temperament like mine, so inclined to be discouraged by the *laissez-faire* spirit of our age. In her personal tradition of elegance, Mme Bricard seemed to personify that motto which I already wanted to take for my own: *I will maintain*.

Besides my two counsellors, I needed someone to act as an intermediary between my own '*bureau de rêveries*' – as the eighteenth century called it – and the workrooms where my ideas would be incarnated in the shape of dresses. At the house of the decorator, Georges Geffroy, then a designer at Patou, I had been lucky enough to meet Mme Marguerite, whom I always think of as Dame Fashion in person. She has the delicate colouring of a Renoir, and over the years she has become part of myself – of my 'dressmaking' self, if I can so call it. Impulsive and obstinate, quick-tempered and patient, she is so much in love with her work that our partnership has had the character of a grand passion. If the world came to an end while she was poring over a dress, I really do not believe she would notice it.

Nothing is ever beautiful enough, or perfect enough, for her. She will stitch, unstitch, cut, cut again, a hundred times; everyone will be made to take a hand, including myself, and still she will not be satisfied. Her enthusiasm mounts as the collection nears completion, and reaches its peak when the models attain that degree of 'finish' which makes us exclaim at last, after we have made twenty last-minute alterations:

'It's impossible to believe that they are the work of human hands!'

Mme Marguerite was exactly the sort of person I needed – someone whose love of clothes equalled my own. She was then working for Patou and was one of the pillars of the establishment, but fortunately the prospect of a change of scene and the desire – strange in one who knew so much – to learn still more about *haute couture* – tempted her away. Conscious that I had acquired a real prize in my new *première*, or workroom forewoman, I created the post of *directrice technique* specially for her, which extended her sphere to the whole of Maison Dior, rather than confining it to one particular room.

In order to explain the exact nature of her new position, I must give a brief sketch of the history of *haute couture* since the years before the 1914 war. If the *couturiers* of today can be compared to stage managers, in the time of Paquin and Doucet they were more like film producers, and their role consisted of exploiting and carrying out the ideas of others.

Of course they needed to have an unerring critical sense in order to choose among the *toiles* produced by the *premières*, and the sketches of the freelance designers who went from house to house displaying the samples of their work which today are still called *gravures*. But just as the individual dress was the work of many different hands – the skirt, sleeve, and bodice were each entrusted to a different person – the collection itself was the work of a multitude of different workrooms and designers, inspired by secret jealousies. Only the personal taste of the head of the house existed to give a certain unity to an otherwise heterogeneous assembly of garments. The success of a dress depended upon the quality of the workmanship, attention to detail, and above all on the beauty of the material. Unlike today, the actual design of the dress might remain virtually unchanged for several seasons.

This system also meant that at the beginning of this century fashions varied little from house to house: and in order to introduce some variety into the dresses, they were often loaded with trimmings of exquisite craftsmanship. Braid, beads, embroidery, lace, and frills, all helped to differentiate models which cut alone would not have distinguished one from the other. Let us assume that each client wanted to wear an exclusive dress, that Mme X could not sport the same *toilette* as her friend Mme Y, and above all not the same as the celebrated and notorious Mlle Z, whose goings-on were the talk of the town; it was physically impossible to design a different dress for each lady, so that the basic design remained the same, and only the trimmings were changed.

With the coming of Paul Poiret all this was altered.

This great artist excelled at creation and decoration: although he was unfortunately an extremely poor business man and was reduced to poverty at the end of his life. Before setting up on his own he had worked at Doucet as a designer: he used to take the material in his hands, drape it softly round the figure of his mannequin, without worrying too much about how it fell, to produce an astonishing colour effect: then a snip here and there with the scissors, a few pins, and the dress was ready!

With their bold curving lines, like the dresses in a Boldini picture, his models were vigorous sketches, whereas the fussy *toilettes* of his predecessors had been carefully painted miniatures. Ornaments and elaborate needlework were out; Iribe's new pink supplanted the Pompadour's pink, and lamé, showing strong Oriental influence, dethroned the eighteenth-century brocades.

The Oriental and Persian influences which inspired Poiret to such an extent had been made fashionable in turn by Sarah Bernhardt and the Russian Ballet. As if they had foreseen the cataclysmic effects of the 1914 war, the artists were busy revolutionizing everything. However, the birth of Cubism passed unnoticed by the simpering ladies of Helleu and Boldini, who were busy exchanging their petticoats for hobble-skirts. The figure of the elegant woman was no longer corseted, but gracefully, and cunningly, shackled.

The fashionable ideal of the odalisque, or hieratic princess of Oriental legends, was given its supreme expression by Ida Rubinstein, dressed by Bakst. Paris in 1912 was like a harem with Paul Poiret as the chic and awe-inspiring sultan. But Orientalism was already on the way out: the only concession which the celebrated courtesan Forzane made to it was her Afghan hound. Paul Oribe, Marty, Lepape, all the designers of Lucien Vogel's fashion magazine *Gazette du Bon Ton*, went mad about the Directoire style, which later merged with Byzantium, Baghdad, Cubism, and Fauvism to compose the famous *Arts Déco* style of 1925.

It was Madeleine Vionnet and Jeanne Lanvin who finally transformed the profession of *couturier*, by executing the dresses in their collections with their own hands and scissors. The model became a whole and at last skirt and bodice were cut according to the same principle. Madeleine Vionnet achieved wonders in this direction: she was a genius at employing her material, and invented the famous cut on the cross which gave the dresses of the women between the two wars their softly moulded look. Freed from the trimmings of 1900 and the decorative motifs of Poiret, dresses now depended entirely on their cut.

This was the age of the great *couturiers*: outstanding among them was Mlle Chanel, who dominated all the rest (although she prided herself on not understanding how to use a needle!). In her personality as well as in her taste, she had style, elegance, and authority. From quite different points of view, she and Madeleine Vionnet can claim to be the creators of modern fashion.

Thus today, after a long period of practically anonymous workmanship, *haute couture* has become the expression of a single personality: that of the head of the house. Perhaps that explains why *couture* and *couturiers* are discussed today more than ever before.

Back to Mme Marguerite, and the special new position I created for her. Being my own designer, I had no need for anyone to stand in for me on that side of the business, but I did need someone to look after the technical side, that is to say, to supervise the workrooms. The *premières* and their staff were capable of producing admirable and minutely detailed workmanship, but their outlook was naturally a little limited, because they lacked the necessary detachment. This detached view was to be provided by Mme Marguerite as my *directrice technique*: armed with my sketches, she was to supervise their execution, and correct any mistake in the cotton canvas *toiles* before they were actually shown to me. It would then only remain for me to make my own personal corrections, which would emphasize the trend of the particular dress, as I had originally conceived it.

Eventually I had to acquire a second *directrice technique*, as my business expanded and Mme Marguerite's responsibilities became too heavy. Raymonde had often praised Mme Linzeler to me for her understanding of *couture*, and at the right moment she proved free to come to us. I gave her a number of different jobs to do, before finally entrusting to her the task of preserving the style and quality of the model in its passage between the studio and the copies demanded by the clients. With her calm appearance and silvery hair, she has the *premières* well in control, and she inspires confidence in the most vacillating client.

Finding the right *premières* for my workroom was like a treasure hunt, for this was the time when the *couturiers' salons* were being invaded by a rather undesirable *clientèle*, buying abundantly with money made on the black market. Eventually I did succeed in acquiring a staff with the right technical skill and knowledge, and I was ready to go before M. Boussac with the nucleus of my organization.

I told him frankly that the organization which I was proposing was on rather a large scale for a house of such modest size, whose models were to be aimed at a fairly restricted *clientèle*. But my goal was perfection, and I needed first-class weapons to achieve it. Fortunately M. Boussac realized that he was dealing with a conscientious craftsman, not a megalomaniac.

When Maison Christian Dior first opened, it had three workrooms in the attics of 30 avenue Montaigne, a tiny studio, a *salon* in which to show the dresses, a *cabine* or dressing-room for the mannequins, an office, and six small fitting-rooms. I employed sixty people all told.

By general agreement, and to my great relief, I was not troubled with the purely administrative side of the business: this was taken over by Jacques Rouet. He had no previous experience of the fashion world, but I liked him, and felt complete confidence in him from the beginning. His role was to provide my castles in the air with solid foundations: when we first met, I painted a gloomy picture to him of the difficulties he would encounter – the inevitable disorder where it would be his duty to bring about order, the inevitable atmosphere of strife where it would be his duty to bring about peace, in short all the delightful confusion which by his very nature the *couturier* cannot help producing.

Fortunately his innate sensitivity enabled him to avoid all the unexpected pitfalls laid for him by *premières*, workers, mannequins, *vendeuses*, journalists, and clients alike. He managed to please all these charming but exacting ladies without giving way to them too much, and appeared to enjoy working for us at the same time. For months he toiled night and day putting to rights the administrative side of a business which was scarcely established before it began to expand rapidly.

Once I had settled both the creative and the administrative side of my business I had to see to the equally vital sales and showing side of it. I realized that the ideal person to look after the sales of the dresses was Suzanne Luling, who came from my native Granville. Although she had never had anything to do with the running of a *couture* house before she came to me, in nine years she has made a great name for herself. It needs the vocabulary of the atomic age to describe her: it is not enough simply to say that she is dynamic, and explosive scarcely conveys her quality. She is never out of sorts, never flags, never lets us down: she rallies the *vendeuses'* spirits when they are sinking, soothes the clients when they are fractious, and infects us all with her buoyant enthusiasm and good sense.

I knew that I could not altogether ignore the goddess of our age – Publicity: and I had been told about a young American called Harrison Elliott, who was anxious to live in France. As the name America is synonymous with publicity, I decided to take him on. His job – at which he excels – consists as much in avoiding an excess of publicity as in stirring it up. It is widely, and quite erroneously, believed that when the house of Christian Dior was launched, enormous sums were spent on publicity: on the contrary in our first modest budget not a single penny was allotted to it. I trusted to the quality of my dresses to get Christian Dior talked about. Moreover, the relative secrecy in which I chose to work aroused a positive whispering campaign, which was excellent (free) propaganda. Gossip, malicious rumours even, are worth more than the most expensive publicity campaign in the world.

Another old friend from Granville came on the scene, in the shape of Serge Heftler-Louiche. Even before the opening of my *couture* house, he had suggested that we should launch Christian Dior perfumes together: and I gladly agreed. When numbers of others of my old friends also wanted to take part in the venture, I was pleased to discover that I was going to be one of the few prophets who was honoured in his own country!

The first *vendeuse* I engaged – Nicole Riotteau – also came from Granville: she had been like a sister to me. I was delighted to see so many old friends reunited, although a very different prospect faced us now from the picnics, fishing expeditions, and croquet-parties of our youth.

Many of the other *vendeuses* who chose to throw in their lot with me had been obliged to leave Paris, and the world of fashion, during the war, and had not yet won back their places in the houses which had employed them in 1939. These were our 'founder members', and pillars of the new house of Christian Dior. With affection and gratitude I recall their names: Yvonne Laget, who combined personal charm with a keen commercial sense: Suzanne Beguin, who had been trained in the great traditions of Mainbocher; Mme Gervais, particularly knowledgeable about Italy; Mme de Segonza and Mme Lancien, two society women who quickly became excellent professional *vendeuses*; and finally the last recruit from Granville, Mme de Nabat, who joined us from Chanel in our second season.

It was never particularly easy engaging the right mannequins, and I chose a peculiarly unfortunate time to try. In despair at not being able to find the type of girl I wanted, I decided to put an advertisement in the paper. As luck would have it, I chose the exact moment when a new law was forcing certain famous Paris brothels to close down, and many of their former inmates were finding themselves without regular employment. These ladies read my advertisement and were overjoyed: perhaps they imagined that a fashion house opening discreetly in a modest house in the avenue Montaigne would conceal some altogether more disreputable trade within its sober walls! On the appointed day, my house, where work was already under way, was literally invaded by unmistakable cohorts of ladies of the streets. Mme Raymonde, who was in charge of the applicants, was appalled, and wondered what on earth to do with them all. I decided I must see the whole lot. From Toulouse-Lautrec downwards, I found myself interviewing every good-time girl in Paris: several of them were actually very pretty, but none of them had the sort of looks suited to my purpose. Amongst this horde, I did discover one charming and rather shy young girl, of an altogether different calibre; she was a former secretary called Marie-Thérèse and she became one of our best models.

After this unfortunate experience, I made up my mind not to risk inserting another advertisement in the paper, and put my staff on to the job of finding the five girls we needed for the opening by other means. In the end my first *cabine* of mannequins contained Noëlle, Paule, Yolande, Lucile, Tania, and Marie-Thérèse. These were the girls who modelled the New Look, and whose graceful pirouetting walk founded a new fashion in modelling. But of that, more later.

By the time I had made all these arrangements, it was July 1946. I decided to open my house on December 15, and show my first collection to the world in the spring of 1947. Before I left Lelong, I gave a small party for my former colleagues, which for me at least, was tinged with sadness: I was bidding farewell to my 'years of apprenticeship', and in the very middle of the dinner I received another unpleasant intimation that my carefree youth was over. I was called to the telephone to hear that my father had died suddenly, in his house at Callian in the south of France. Although I was then forty, I felt as if I had come of age for the second time.

However impatient we get when our parents refuse to accept the fact that we have grown up, this very weakness of theirs supports and comforts us – how much we only realize when we are suddenly faced with their loss. I was no longer a child to anyone: it was my turn to provide comfort and support for those who were coming after me. I had to step out of the warmth and intimacy of the family circle and welcome into the world that forbidding stranger – Christian Dior, *couturier*.

I certainly did my best to provide him with an attractive dwelling: and in order that he might share as much of my past as possible, I chose to decorate his *couture* house in the colours which had dominated my Parisian childhood, and had since gone completely out of fashion. From 1900 to 1914 decoration *à la Louis Seize* was all the rage in the 'new' houses in Passy: white woodwork, white enamelled furniture, grey hangings, glass doors with square panes and bronze light brackets with small lampshades. The unobtrusive elegance of this period still survives in the *salons* of the Ritz and Plaza, and the house of Cheruit was decorated in it; I felt that it would be the ideal background against which to show my collections, with its sober but by no means bleak simplicity, above all its classical and Parisian elegance. I was determined that my decor should not degenerate into elaborate decorations and distract the eye from my clothes, which should after all be the focal point of the whole proceedings.

But where, in 1946, was I to find the man capable of transforming my dreams into reality, within the limits of my modest budget? My friends who were professional decorators were either too purist or too much in love with their ideas to listen to mine: I did not want an authentic Louis Seize interior – I wanted a 1910 version of Louis Seize, a notion which most of them would have considered mere folly.

I remembered that Victor Grandpierre, whom I had seen a lot of in Cannes, at the beginning of the German occupation, had often told me that he wanted to become a decorator. He was the son of the fashionable architect who built Princess de Polignac's house, Jean de Reszke's private theatre, and several other masterpieces of the 1910 period. Victor Grandpierre had been brought up in the right traditions: and he did in fact prove to be the very man I was looking for.

I sent such a pressing letter to him at Cannes, where he was on holiday, that he instantly left for Paris, and set to work trying to put into practice the very confused ideas which I sketched out to him. Fortunately our tastes coincided wonderfully, and we were both equally happy recapturing the magic years of our childhood. He created the 'Helleu' *salon* of my dreams: all in white and pearl grey, looking very Parisian with its crystal chandeliers and profusion of quintias palms, so much prettier than the bizarre philodendron which is in vogue today.

After completing the *salon*, Victor created the tiny *boutique* which I intended to be a copy of the eighteenth-century shops which sold luxurious trifles. While he was still at work, that arbiter of elegance, Christian Bérard, paid us a visit of inspection. With his beard flowing, and his little dog Jacinthe at his heels, he penetrated every corner of the house. We awaited his verdict with beating hearts, knowing his pronouncements on matters of taste and style to be infallible. Fortunately he gave us his approval, and suggested several improvements of detail such as covering the *boutique* in *toile de Joy* and lavishly scattering about hatboxes inscribed with our name on the tops of cupboards and in odd corners. It was an inspiration: the seeming casualness brought the whole place to life.

Carried away by the subject of my decorative schemes, I have said nothing about my actual feelings at the moment when I presented to the public the first dresses bearing my name. I must confess that of all my collections, the opening one caused me the least effort and worry. Then I ran no risk of disappointing my public, because I had no public to disappoint: nothing was known about me and therefore nothing expected of me. Of course I had to try to please them – but more for the sake of my own self-respect than anything else. Far from wanting to revolutionize fashion, I was chiefly concerned with producing a high standard of workmanship. I aimed at being considered a good craftsman – no mean aim, it is true, since it implies both integrity and high quality – but I never guessed what an explosive quality my modest formula would prove to have in an age of compromise and *laissez-faire*.

I left Lelong on December 1 and went to stay with my friends the Colles at Fleury-en-Bière, in the middle of the Forest of Fontainebleau, which was then under snow. I spent a fortnight there, creating and designing my first collection. Although it is true, as is often said, that one breathes in fashion with the very air of Paris, I find that the peace and calm of the country is absolutely essential to me after a while, in order to reflect on the lessons which I have learnt in the city itself. A thousand fleeting images surged through my mind, and were speedily imprisoned by the strokes of my pencil, lest they elude me for ever. One by one I weeded them out: I pondered on the ideas which remained for several days before making my final choice, which was the basis of the New Look.

Temperamentally I am reactionary, not to be confused with retrograde. We were just emerging from a poverty-stricken, parsimonious era, obsessed with ration books and clothes-coupons: it was only natural that my creations should take the form of a reaction against this dearth of imagination. I suppose it was inevitable that certain people should say that I designed those long full dresses, with an immense yardage of material in their skirts, which were the triumph of my collection and are fashionable today, in response to pressure from M. Boussac and his textile interests. But they made a great mistake in thinking that fashion varies according to the dictates of commerce: I swear that any fashion inspired by that sort of consideration would have no chance of surviving, still less of succeeding and developing. In fact, M. Boussac gave me an absolutely free hand to design as I pleased.

In December 1946, as a result of the war and uniforms, women still looked and dressed like Amazons. But I designed clothes for flowerlike women, with rounded shoulders, full feminine busts, and hand-span waists above enormous spreading skirts. An ethereal appearance is only achieved by elaborate workmanship: in order to satisfy my love of architecture, and clear-cut design, I wanted to employ quite a different technique in fashioning my clothes, from the methods then in use – I wanted them to be constructed like buildings. Thus I moulded my dresses to the curves of the female body, so that they called attention to its shape. I emphasized the width of the hips, and gave the bust its true prominence; and in order to give my models more 'presence' I lined nearly all of them with cambric or taffeta, thus reverting to an old tradition.

My return to long-forgotten techniques aroused a host of difficulties, for of course none of my staff had any experience of them. As soon as I had exhibited my designs, they applied themselves to the problem, with Mme Marguerite at their head. The work was carried out under conditions of unbelievable difficulty. The lack of space in my studio – formerly a boudoir – forced us to make use of every inch of free space in order to have enough elbow room. Eventually I fled from the growing invasion of materials on to the landing, and even found myself working on the steps of the staircase. The whole building was in a fever. One of our key *premières* collapsed with a nervous breakdown, a victim of this mad regime; we had to replace her in the midst of the battle by a particularly talented underling, Monique, who luckily was more than equal to the task. With Christiane, she deserves every credit for the success of the collection. They even had to make the suits, because the expert whom I engaged for the purpose proved incapable of doing it.

My own thoughts and energies were concentrated on the most perfect reproduction of the ninety models I had designed. All around me, at the orders of Mme Marguerite, the *premières* and their subordinates were rediscovering or inventing the appropriate technique to execute the designs which had been entrusted to them. They were mostly complete strangers to one another, but within a few weeks, they were working together as proper teams.

Worn out by the triple task of organizing the business, recruiting the staff, and creating the dresses, I sometimes let myself flop down exhausted on to the heaps of material. By now there was practically nowhere else to sit.

We all felt the strain. There were only six mannequins and the thousands of different fittings imposed such a nervous and physical strain upon them that on one occasion an extremely pretty blonde English girl turned faint and collapsed into my arms. I thought I was clutching her securely, but she continued to slide to the floor – and I found myself holding ... her bust! I had completely forgotten that in my desire to give prominence to this most feminine attribute, I had asked those whom nature had neglected, to equip themselves with 'falsies'.

The materials themselves were another source of worry. In those days there was nothing like the high standards of quality we have today. I wanted silk fabrics where the yarn itself and not the woven material had been dyed – but anything which had any body to it was extremely hard to find. For years, crêpe romain, georgette, muslin, and clinging jersey had supplanted taffeta, faille, duchesse satin, and wool taffeta.

Inexorably, the date at which I would have to show my collection crept forward. I intentionally had not worried about publicity but trusted to a few loyal friends to get the new house talked about in Paris. The intellectual and social standing of Comte Étienne de Beaumont and Mme Larivière, and the fervour which Marie-Louise Bousquet, Christian Bérard, and several friends of mine who were journalists, including Michel de Brunhoff, Paul Caldagues, and James de Coquet, managed to communicate to others, aroused a fever of popular curiosity, from which, all at once, I recoiled in alarm. I felt that too many hopes were being pinned on me, and that I was incapable of fulfilling them.

It was only with the greatest possible reluctance that I was finally persuaded to show my dresses to my friends one evening just before their formal presentation to the public. Bérard cried out that I had achieved a miracle, and Marie-Louise Bousquet chimed in with other flattering exclamations. Being superstitious by nature, I immediately looked round for a piece of wood to touch: it all seemed a little too good to be true, and therefore ominous.

But my most fortunate piece of publicity was quite unplanned: *Life* magazine asked me to pose with a smile and the supposed 'natural' or 'inspired' expression, which I have had to try and assume so often since. At the time I had no idea of the importance of an article in *Life* in launching anything. Like Fortune, the goddess of Publicity often seems to smile most favourably on those who court her least.

Up till now I had only held hasty rehearsals, in a *salon* cluttered up with mannequins, seamstresses, and *premières*: but it was essential to have some sort of a dress rehearsal. Nevertheless I knew it would give absolutely no idea of the collection as it would ultimately appear to the public: until the opening, the true significance of the dresses would be lost on anyone except those who had actually created and sewn them. So I decided not even to show the models to the *vendeuses*. For them, as for the Press and my future *clientèle*, the curtain would rise on the collection for the first time on the appointed day. I have stuck to this decision ever since, in spite of the pleas which have been made to me to yield. I suppose I am subconsciously trying to halt the invasions of the commercial spirit into the *milieu* which I love.

At last the finishing touches were put to the dresses. Now that there was no further opportunity to alter them, I suddenly felt a strange calm come over me. I had only one thing to say about my collection – I thought it 'would do', that is to say, I thought it would please and satisfy the *clientèle* at which it was aimed.

Fortunately the anxiety of receiving my guests correctly took my mind off my actual collection. By a miracle the decor was finished, as in spite of my constant nagging the decorators had lagged behind their schedule. As Mme Delahaye had predicted, the last bang of the last hammer was actually heard as the first visitor entered.

I myself arrived very early on the great day and fidgeted about on the carpet which was still being tacked down. By dawn, the whole house was in a state of uproar which made it seem more like late afternoon. Carmen Colle had spent the last hours of darkness transforming the cubbyhole, which was supposed to be our *boutique*, into a proper little miniature shop. In the *salon*, Lachaume was arranging the last vases of flowers, and I thought the curtains and hangings of grey satin made it look very elegant. In the dressing-room, the mannequins were ready for the fray, and by a miracle all the models seemed to be there too, having arrived safely from the workrooms.

At 10.30, with the *salons* full to bursting, the first mannequin showed the first dress. Marie-Thérèse, half dead with fright, stumbled at her first appearance, collapsed in tears, and was henceforth incapable of showing a dress. Very soon, the entry of each model was accompanied by gusts of applause. I stuffed my ears, terrified of feeling confident too soon; but a series of short bulletins from the field of battle confirmed to me that my troops – led, flags flying, by my star mannequin, the inimitable Tania – had triumphed.

Now the last dress had been shown, amid a tumult of enthusiasm, and Mme Marguerite, Mme Bricard, and I stood gazing at each other in the dressing-room. We were none of us able to speak. Then Raymonde came to look for us, crying with joy, in order to propel us into the big *salon*, where we were greeted by a salvo of applause. As long as I live, whatever triumphs I win, nothing will ever exceed my feelings at that supreme moment.

— 3 —

THE NEW LOOK

Very soon the public, the Press, and my sales ledger, combined to tell me that, like M. Jourdain in *Le Bourgeois Gentilhomme*, who spoke prose without knowing it, I had done a 'Dior' without realizing it. The style which was being universally hailed as new and original, was nothing but the sincere and natural expression of fashion, which I had always sought to achieve. It happened that my own inclinations coincided with the tendency of the times and thus attained added importance. It is easy to make oneself look ridiculous by injecting philosophy and reflections on society into the midst of a discussion on silks and satins, but since I am widely held responsible for a social trend, I may perhaps be allowed to analyse my own success.

I believe it was due to the fact that I brought back the neglected art of pleasing.

Remember the years before the war. Remember the extravagance of those surrealist trimmings – in tune with the surrealist interior decoration of the houses – with which Mme Schiaparelli loved to decorate her clothes. An evening dress might look like a huge lobster, and a hat would be made in the shape of a shoe or a cutlet – as for the buttons, heaven knows what shape they were! It was fine just so long as it was the fashion, for fashion is always right – it has a fundamental rightness which those who create it, like those who follow it, often know nothing about.

With her great talent, Mme Schiaparelli knew how to push the frontiers of elegance until it bordered on the bizarre. Perhaps, from 1938 onwards, even she went a little too far, because Balenciaga, who had just opened his house, Mainbocher, and Robert Piguet, with whom I was then working as a designer, initiated the return to a more classical style. With its restrictions and the *zazou* fashions which I discussed earlier, the war quickly put a stop to this natural development. But in 1947, after so many years of wandering, *couture* was weary of only catering for painters and poets, and wanted to revert to its true function, of clothing women and enhancing their beauty.

In the opinion of the public, this was exactly the function which my first collection performed. They were delighted to be faced with fashions which were European rather than exotic, clothes which were well made and styles which were becoming and pretty for the first time in years. In 1947 it was time for fashion to forsake adventure and make a temporary return to base.

You will remember that I was aiming principally at an established *clientèle* of experienced buyers and habitually elegant women: I now had the pleasant surprise of finding that young women wanted to adopt the new fashion as well. Dominique Blanchard, in the full bloom of her youthful beauty, wore the most ostentatiously New Look dress in her part in a play of Giraudoux (*l'Apollon de Bellac*). I liked this model so much that I christened it 'Chérie'. It had a tight bodice, a tiny waist, and eighty yards of pleated white faille descending almost to the hem in the enormous bustle of the skirt.

Saint-Germain des Près did not want to be left out, and I was delighted to find the existentialist singer, Juliette Gréco, who incarnated black-jerseyed, tight-trousered youth, within the precincts of a house of *couture*. With rare intelligence, Juliette Gréco understood how to conciliate the demands of her own individual style with those of my designs. Thus the New Look became symbolic of youth and the future.

My first collection was successful beyond my wildest dreams. From the moment it opened, the Press and then the buyers packed into my *salons*. The crowds forced us to enlarge the landing, and get rid of a charming old staircase. There was still not enough room, so the invaders spilled out on to the staircase, and people sat on the steps in order of precedence, like in an amphitheatre. We soon found that we were having to turn people away every day, so we instituted a system of reserved places, which prevented people from feeling that they had been deliberately excluded as a result of a personal grudge on the part of the management. This system had another advantage, in that it enabled the public to get in and prevented would-be copyists from keeping out potential clients.

It was my first contact with the fashion journalists and professional buyers. At Piguet or Lelong, where I was only a designer, I vanished from sight once my dresses had been created. Once my task was accomplished, I was off to enjoy peace and quiet in the country, and relax after the turbulence of preparing the collection. Now everything was different. I had to follow up my astonishingly successful opening, which involved me in fresh responsibilities.

Of course I had several old friends among the Press. I have already mentioned Michel de Brunhoff, manager of French *Vogue*, Paul Caldagues, and Lucien and Cosette Vogel of the *Jardin des Modes*, who had helped me in my career. When I was a designer, I had known Alice Chavanne and Genevieve Perreau of *Figaro*. In the days when Mme Jacques Bousquet held a *salon* in her little house in the rue Boissière, I often went along on her 'day'. This was long before the period of the place du Palais Bourbon when this day became celebrated as 'Marie-Louise's Thursday', not only in Paris where it was a famous rallying-point, but all over the world. I was extremely shy in those days, and never penetrated beyond Marie-Louise's facade of unvarying affability, which is her protection against the encroachments of the world. Later, work, the friends we had in common, as well as the joys and sorrows which we shared, enabled me to see behind the smiling mask. She became a great friend and ally of mine, and just before the war introduced me to Carmel Snow, who had intended to ask me to do designs for *Harper's Bazaar*.

At Lelong I had known Bettina Wilson, now Bettina Ballard, who was then working for *Vogue*. Some time before my first show, I had also met Mr Perkins, of the all-important American magazine *Woman's Wear*. This paper finds sufficient interest in the subject of feminine apparel to distribute fifty pages daily of editorials and advertisements on fashion across the whole of America! I also knew Mme Castanie, who presides over the bible of French fashion, *Officiel de la Couture*, and Lucie Noel of the *New York Herald*. But I still had many vital contacts with the Press to make, to say nothing of the all-important photographers and artists. The relationship of a *couturier* with the Press is like a love affair – a never-ending love affair, renewed each season, involving endless intrigues and reconciliations. Elliott was doing the work of ten men, and even so could not cope with the extraordinary variety of demands which were made upon his time by the Press so I had to see its principal representatives personally.

I also began to experience for myself the remorseless war which the daily papers carry on in order to reveal as early as possible the fashion secrets of the coming season to their readers. A house which is determined to get as good a Press as possible, also knows that premature and detailed publication of its models helps to produce copies and vulgarizes the style. So I had to learn how to fend off indiscreet questions with a wary smile. I had to extend a warm welcome to all the world, appear to be delighted at seeing so many of my models reproduced, and at the same time feel furious if too many were. Of course the *couturier* to whom the magazines give too little space is not satisfied either. The general public is happily ignorant of the storm of suspicion and ill feeling to which a reproduction of a model in colour on the cover of a fashion magazine can give rise. The number of models from each *couturier* which are reproduced, their position and juxtaposition in the paper – all these details are eagerly noted by his rivals. Rightly or wrongly, *couturiers* are quick to suspect favouritism and are as susceptible to affront as the authors of plays, which is saying a lot!

Having made the necessary contacts with the Press, I now had to meet the professional buyers and their backers. As the date of my opening had been comparatively late in the season, a good many of the American buyers had already left Paris, after placing all their orders. But the furore created by the first collection of the new *couture* house induced them to return. I knew practically none of them personally, though of course some of their names were familiar to me – Magnin, Harry Blum, Hattie Carnegie, the once celebrated representatives of Bergdorf Goodman, Miss Frankau and Miss Daude, Leon Schmodlen, who represented Bendel, and Miss Cathlin, the buyer at Marshall Field.

In 1945, the buyers who had gradually torn themselves away from Chanel and Vionnet in 1918, were turning their steps once more in the direction of Paris. But times had changed. The big shops they represented now only stocked a line of made-to-measure dresses for the sake of prestige – and at a heavy loss. *Couture*, in the Parisian sense, scarcely exists in America, the land where it has taken all the undoubted talents of Mainbocher, Valentine, Charlie James, and others merely to keep themselves in existence. I knew therefore that we could not hope for the lavish orders by the hundred which our predecessors had enjoyed; but only carefully premeditated orders, limited to the models which were either most typical of the new fashion, or easiest to reproduce.

It was true that I was a French *couturier*, but I had to understand the needs of elegant women all over the world as well as my fellow countrywomen. Helped by my good relations with such experienced members of my profession, I was soon designing prints for California and muslins for Rio de Janeiro, in an effort to give women of different ways of life the clothes they wanted.

Maison Dior was in a ferment, even at night. As a newcomer to the world of *haute couture*, I had now to catch up on my start, and sell, sell, sell, my models all day long. Fortunately the whole world was marching in my direction, following the vanguard of the critics. The English followed the Americans; then came the Italians who were excellent clients from the first, giving the lie to this absurd myth of a Franco-Italian fashion war, which does not exist, and never has. The Belgians, the Swiss, and the Scandinavians followed. A little while after came the South Americans, the Australians, and several seasons later, the Germans and the Japanese.

Our *vendeuses* were up to their ears in work, for now private clients were swelling the throng of indefatigable professionals, and there was danger of a complete bottleneck in the workrooms. I decided to open two more at once, and M. Boussac and I also committed ourselves to the construction of a new seven-storey building of workrooms in spite of the difficulties. Our principal problem was finding a site on which to build: there seemed nothing for it but to knock down the old stables, and I felt that it was probably the first time in the career of this great horse-lover that he had ever consented to such a sacrilege!

Where was the small exclusive house of my dreams now? I was slightly overcome by the consequences of my sudden rise to fame and inclined to regret the transformation of my original modest conception into something so much vaster. All the same, I was human enough to enjoy being a success and, after all, presumably the aim of one's labours is to succeed, so I had no legitimate grievance! I must hasten to say that all my pleasure arose from the fact that my dresses were being appreciated by the public, and the hard work of the little community at avenue Montaigne was therefore rewarded. I disliked intensely the other side of the picture: the inevitable gossip, true or untrue, which was retailed about me, and the sly curious whispers which my presence aroused whenever I was recognized in public.

It was Christian Bérard who provided the fitting climax of my triumphant first season, in the course of a dinner given by Marie-Louise Bousquet. Bébé had done me a pastel drawing of the house in avenue Montaigne, which I henceforth had reproduced on everything from Christmas cards to the programmes of the collection. At the dinner, he proposed a wonderful improvised toast to me, which summed up all the vigour of his own philosophy of life:

'My dear Christian,' he concluded. 'Savour this moment of happiness well, for it is unique in your career. Never again will success come to you so easily: for tomorrow begins the anguish of living up to, and if possible, surpassing yourself.'

At the time I listened to his words without taking in their meaning. The poison of success had not yet had time to work in my veins. But very soon Bérard was to be proved right, as usual.

At last I was free to take a holiday, and let mind and body recover from the exhausting effects of the past few months. I set off for the Touraine, rejoicing in my liberty. Although this was 1947, France had taken a long time to lick her wounds and it still seemed like wartime in the country. Tanks had broken the surface of the roads, which had not yet been mended. I am irretrievably bored by everything mechanical, so that I have never learnt to drive. As I had never been rich enough to employ a chauffeur, I had never had a car of my own. Fortunately Suzanne Luling offered to lend me her gallant little Simca, because cars were not to be had in those days, and a friend of mine suggested that he should drive me. The Simca had only escaped being requisitioned by both French and Germans by a series of cunning stratagems. Now it was brought proudly out of retirement, that is to say it got as far as the garage door. It then occurred to me that this wonder car had possibly been spared because it was not worth a brass farthing to anyone: with old tyres and an asthmatic engine, it advanced painfully in a series of noisy bursts. Every hundred miles we came to a stand-still – there had been a puncture in one of the tyres, so the tyre had to be mended and blown up. Off we went again, only to find two hours later that there had been another puncture, and the procedure had to be repeated. All the same, I felt I was bowling along in a triumphal chariot.

In this manner, we did eventually reach the Touraine, where I lived on the fat of the land for a month. I was thankful to find that my face was unknown, and that I was to be spared the autograph books, in which I could never think of anything to write. I toured the small hotels of the district, enjoying the old-fashioned *cuisine* which, in spite of food shortages, acquitted itself with honour. After so many lean years, I had practically forgotten what it felt like to live well.

It was a wonderful holiday: I felt that those little towns, those country churches, and those well-tended gardens, even the smell of simmering stew on the hob, epitomized the France I loved. I went for long walks on foot, and in the evenings either played patience or read my favourite tomes of historical memoirs. But every night I put through a call to Paris, to keep in touch with what had happened during the day, and to follow the dizzy rise of prices – I suppose my Norman blood prevents me ever really forgetting completely about my work.

Even the pleasantest of holidays must come to an end sometime. The Simca breathed its last in full view of the tower at Dourdain, so I rang up Paris to hire a car. Christian Dior, the public figure, now came into his own. He was photographed from every angle. I reflected philosophically that it was the price of fame: but apart from my dislike of the whole business, I could not help thinking that I cut a sorry figure – a well-fed gentleman in the Parisian's favourite neutral-coloured suit – compared with the glamorous, not to say dandified or effeminate *couturier* of the popular imagination.

I wondered if I ought to transform myself, in order not to disappoint my public? Perhaps I ought to go on a diet, and renounce not only greed, but everything which made life worth living.

I splashed out timidly with a flower in my buttonhole. I ordered several more suits from my tailor, put myself in the hands of a masseur, and almost immediately gave the whole project up. I decided that the gap between imagination and reality was too wide. With relief, I sank back into my own shell, which had come to fit me very comfortably after so many years.

I was in the midst of working for my second collection (the winter collection, to be presented in July) when I received a letter from an American fashion house called Neiman Marcus, inviting me to come to Dallas, Texas, to receive an Oscar. The very idea of such a journey, to what sounded like the ends of the earth, struck terror into me, and my first instinct was to refuse at once. But the idea of getting to know America was too tempting to be resisted. My biggest buyers had been Americans, and I wanted to see the American women who were wearing my clothes in their natural surroundings. Re-reading the letter, I discovered that the Oscar had been instituted during the war and this was the first time it had been awarded to a French *couturier*. I had won this honour with my very first collection.

Curiosity and pride alone would not have been enough to send me across the Atlantic. What really spurred me on was the feeling that it was the revival of French *couture* which was being honoured through me. It was my duty to reaffirm the ancient supremacy of Paris in the field of fashion, and represent my profession and my country at the same time.

I could not set off until I had presented my second collection, and so I set to work with renewed energy. The anxiety which Bérard had prophesied gnawed at me, but far from paralysing me, it inspired me to fresh heights. It was a crazy collection of immensely wide, immensely long skirts, the New Look pushed to extremes. Dresses took up a fantastic yardage of material, and this time went right down to the ankles. Girls could safely feel that they had all the trappings of a fairy-tale princess to wear. A golden age seemed to have come again. War had passed out of sight and there were no other wars on the horizon. What did the weight of my sumptuous materials, my heavy velvets and brocades, matter? When hearts were light, mere fabrics could not weigh the body down. Abundance was still much too much of a novelty for a poverty cult to develop out of inverted snobbism.

We were dizzy with success, and nearly involved ourselves in a catastrophe for a totally unexpected reason: there was one simple pink wool dress in the collection, called 'Bonbon', cut according to the new technique of the corolla. This dress created a sensation, partly because it was so pretty, but also, and more to the point, because a mistake had been made in working out the price, and it was fixed at a figure which was considerably less than what it cost us to make. Our clients, of course, made no mistake. They knew a bargain when they saw one. Ruin was just round the corner, for with each reproduction of the dress, our total loss would have increased. Fortunately the disaster was retrievable, and our business was not rocked to its foundations.

I often smile today when I think of the people who talked about Maison Christian Dior then as if it were an established Parisian attraction, like the Eiffel Tower or the Can-Can, and forgot that the firm was exactly six months old.

All this took place in the year of grace 1947. 1937 had danced in the ospreys and furbelows of Schiaparelli, on top of a grumbling volcano. Ten years later, people were dancing in the New Look on a volcano extinguished, we hope, forever. The post-war spirit inspired a series of balls. Christian Bérard organized the 'Panache Ball' where the most elegant heads in the world were decorated with every type of feather, including birds of paradise, ostrich, osprey. The 'Ball of the Birds' followed, where gorgeously plumed masks lent an air of mystery to a pretty face.

Comte Étienne de Beaumont wanted to revive his parties which had been famous before the war. He reopened the doors of his music room for a 'Ball of Kings', at which every celebrity in Paris appeared beneath a cardboard crown, from King Dagobert, to the Queen of Spades and Hearts, via Marie Antoinette and the Queen of Sheba. Marie-Laure de Noailles took up the challenge and at Trou-sur-Lune, the ephemeral royalties transformed themselves into characters typical of the famous French comedian, Jacques Tati. Marie-Louise Bousquet, Arturo Lopez Willshaw, the American Ambassador, and his beautiful wife and I clubbed together to go as the habitués of a bistro.

As if possessed by a frenzy, everybody wanted to give his ball for a particular work, or for his friends, in Paris, in the country, on the Eiffel Tower, on a boat on the Seine, anywhere where it was a novelty to dance. As our friends from abroad poured in to visit us, Paris became cosmopolitan once more. Arturo Lopez Willshaw and his wife, who are as Parisian as if they had been born there, reopened their beautiful house in Neuilly. New faces emerged. A young Portuguese had the charming idea of hiring the Deligny swimming pool, which floats on the Seine, in order to present a Venetian entertainment for his guests. Surrounded with flowers, the swimming pool turned into a dream lake. The glow of the candles, and the ingenious Spanish Moroccan facades erected in wood, reminded me of the Palace of the Doges, while the guests in their dominoes, passing in and out of the airy arcades, were like the characters in a comic opera.

This dance at Deligny was a sort of precursor of the celebrated ball Charles de Besteigui was to give several years later in Venice itself, in his wonderful Palazzo Labia. This was the most marvellous spectacle which I have ever seen, or ever shall see. The splendour of the costumes rivalled the splendid attire of the figures in the Tiepolo frescoes on the walls. There was an enormous crowd round the palace, whose acclamations mingled with the greetings of the guests. The magic of a summer's night in Italy held us in its eternal spell and put us outside time.

How can I express my feelings about fêtes? In an age when it is fashionable to affect to despise luxury and grand entertainments, I will not disguise the fact that the Besteigui ball is a memory which I am proud to possess. Parties like that are genuine works of art: people may be annoyed by them, by the very fact that they are on a grand scale – nevertheless they are desirable, and important even in the history of our time, because they produce the authentic sense of popular enjoyment.

Europe was tired of dropping bombs and now only wanted to let off fireworks. This new lease of *joie de vivre* never succeeded in equalling the frenzies of 1920, whose echoes alone reached me, as I was too young to take part in them. But it was reassuring to find that the coarse feasts of the black-marketeers were being gradually superseded by the more elegant entertainments of smart society. Maison Christian Dior profited from this wave of optimism and the return of an ideal of civilized happiness.

I insist on using the word happiness. I believe Alphonse Daudet once wrote that he wanted his books to make him become a 'merchant of happiness'. In my modest role of *couturier* I pursue the same aim. My first creations were called names like 'Love', 'Tenderness', and 'Happiness'. Women have instinctively understood that I dream of making them not only more beautiful, but also happier. That is why they have rewarded me with their patronage.

There was only one note of melancholy in my grateful paean of triumph. I had to renounce a whole side of my life which had been very dear to me. Henceforth I had to devote myself in earnest to the role of Christian Dior, *couturier*. I rehearsed it with some success during that brilliant season in Paris, before the fateful moment came when I had to take my new personality on tour.

— 4 —

AN INNOCENT ABROAD IN THE U.S.A

In spite of the scorn which my family had poured on the fortune-teller's prophecy that I would travel widely, it had already come true to a certain extent before 1947. But although I had even gone as far afield as Russia (in 1931) I had never left the confines of Europe. To reach Dallas, Texas, I had to cross the ocean, and enter the New World.

I decided to do the thing thoroughly and make a complete tour of the United States. It may not sound a particularly bold venture in these days when people travel huge distances so casually, but the thought of it filled me with trepidation. For one thing, although I was beginning to know my role of *couturier* by heart, I knew very little about this new stage on which I would have to play it. I had seen so many different things about America by so many different people, that I no longer knew whom or what to believe: although of course this very mystery filled me with excitement.

Somewhere behind a composite facade of skyscrapers, grand canyons, Niagara Falls, petrol pumps, huge dusty deserts, and something called the 'Deep South' (created in my mind *malgré moi* by films, magazines, and picture postcards) lay the real America. What would it be like? My ears rang with slogans: 'Hollywood with its film producers and stars is not America', 'The Americans who come to Europe are not the real Americans'. Old Paris friends like the poet Archibald MacLeish and the musician and critic, Virgil Thompson, were not characteristic American types either.

I was told that the American millionaires I might have met were anachronisms, and belonged back in the age of *Gone With the Wind*. Nor could the GIs who liberated us be regarded as true Americans, because everybody knows that men in uniform behave quite unlike themselves.

I gradually formed the picture of a gigantic country, inhabited by an entirely new race of people, of no known characteristics or habits. It was scarcely reassuring! So in order to rally my spirits, I began to dwell on a series of deliberately old-fashioned notions, which, I felt, could scarcely lead to disappointment. I rejected what little I knew of Steinbeck or Hemingway in favour of the early films of Charlie Chaplin, Paul Muni's gangsters, Pearl White, and Mary Pickford; I even went back to Fenimore Cooper in search of a more soothing America.

With this intellectual armour to protect me, I bade my friends good-bye as if I were going on an Arctic expedition, and embarked on the *Queen Elizabeth* at the beginning of September with a heavy heart, encumbered, of course, with a thousand absolutely essential suitcases.

It was the first time I had ever made a trip on a great ocean liner, and as the *Queen Elizabeth* lay in the docks at Cherbourg, she seemed to me more imposing than Mont Blanc itself. But in spite of the hideous style of luxury which she shares with all other big ships, the *Queen Elizabeth* was instantly agreeable to me. I had a spacious cabin and a pleasant steward. Besides which, an English ship reeks of England, and there is no other country in the world, besides my own, whose way of life I like so much. I love English traditions, English politeness, English architecture, I even love English cooking! I dote on Yorkshire pudding, mince pies, stuffed chicken, and above all I worship the English breakfast of tea, porridge, eggs and bacon.

It was in fact by far the most agreeable sea crossing I have ever made. Among the passengers were Ivan Patsevitch, Alex and Tatiana Liberman, and Bettina Ballard; I knew none of them very well when we set off, but by the time we reached New York we were firm friends, and I could not have hoped for a nicer quartet to introduce me to America. In such pleasant company, my habitual shyness melted, and the hours slipped by.

I found I had harboured a completely erroneous impression about life aboard an ocean liner. Here were no haughty elusive cosmopolitan beauties making fleeting appearances in the evening, draped in sables. It is true that the horse-game or lotto-bingo was played in the lounge in the evening, beneath a portrait of the Queen painted by the most official of her official painters, but the people who played, although undoubtedly rich, were neither young nor smart. As a set, they went early to bed, and the only concessions they made to the traditional grandeur of the *Queen Elizabeth* were their rather antiquated dinner jackets and evening dresses.

I for one did not repine at this lack of the gala spirit: it left our little group free for a delightful existence of sunbathing, bridge, and gossip which inevitably centred round New York. But to all my questions, it was the city of New York itself which gave the best answer – when it appeared on the horizon at dawn on the fifth day, radiant in the glory of its Indian summer.

Little by little the first rock of another world – the New World – rose out of the sea. At the top of the rock stood an enormous city, its base still shrouded in darkness, but its summit adorned with numerous towers of Babel, already gilded by the morning sun. The zest for life and self-confidence of the whole nation were perfectly conveyed by those thousand upward-pointing obelisks. Carried away by my enthusiasm, I completely forgot the ancient continent of my birth: how far away now seemed the airy structures of my own Eiffel Tower.

I was recalled to a sense of reality – and mundane problems like my luggage, my tickets, and my visa – by the sirens announcing disembarkation. Men in uniform, from park attendants to Swiss Guards, have always inspired me with mingled respect and fear. In vain did I remind myself that my innocence had been established a dozen times: I still faced the immigration authorities with all the guilt of a stowaway, my head buzzing with stories of their notorious severity. I remembered the absurd questions

I had been asked in Paris, how I had had my fingerprints taken and been forced to swear on oath that I was not a Communist. It was true I nourished no sinister designs against America or her President ... but one never knows.

Having turned out and searched my pockets for my passport, customs declaration, disembarkation card, luggage checks, and vaccination certificates, having found and lost them again several times, having finally managed to grasp the whole lot in my hands, and having discovered the right queue, in which I sat down and stood up twenty-five times in order to advance one yard, I ended up at last with a beating heart in front of an ominously silent gentleman with gold spectacles, who waved me politely to my twenty-sixth seat. He took my papers, he went through innumerable long lists, devoted himself to a minute checking of every conceivable detail, and after asking me how long I intended to spend in America, finally observed, with a knowing wink:

'Well, so you're the designer. What about the skirt length?'

I was convinced that I had departed from the ship shrouded in anonymity; I was also astonished to discover that the immigration authorities were so intimately interested in the length of skirts. I replied in rather bad English that after all I had not made skirts as long as all that, and rose to my feet, overjoyed at having escaped so easily. The New Look had proved an excellent passport for its inventor.

I now began to run after my suitcases, as though the stewards who were carrying them intended to throw them into the sea. I mistook my way in the long corridors, and felt so totally lost that when several microphones started to boom out my name, far from being alarmed, I heaved a sigh of relief:

'Thank heaven,' I cried, on hearing these enormous echoing cries of 'Dior, Dior', 'they've found me at last.'

My satisfaction was short-lived. Once spied and identified, I found myself hustled into the grill-room, without having the least idea what was going on, and faced with an impromptu Press conference. It was my first experience of this ghastly ordeal to which I have since got accustomed. It is like being a prisoner in the dock before a terrible tribunal, with the courtroom filled with flash bulbs firing at you before you even say a word. On this occasion I faced the grave charge of wishing to conceal the sacrosanct legs of the American female, and I had to defend myself on the spot. It seemed that the immigration officer's wink had been anything but benevolent! Fortunately my native Norman caution got me out of a tight corner. Pretending to search for words in my halting English, I looked desperately for a sympathetic face to rescue me. At that very moment, as in all the best melodramas, a late arrival pushed his way through the crowd, and advanced towards me with open arms.

This saviour, sent from heaven at the critical moment, was none other than Nicolas Bongard, a friend of twenty years' standing, who had married an American girl and settled down in New York after the war, combining with Jean Schlumberger to launch a jewellery business of exquisite taste. He knew his America, and had no doubt at all about what was in store for me: braving the rules, he had climbed aboard the boat to come to my assistance. Thus strengthened, I took heart and began to reply to my bombardment of questions.

My two days in New York were spent in a continuous state of wonder. The electric air of the city kept me constantly on the go and I tried to keep my eyes wide open the whole time, in order to miss nothing of my first impressions of so striking a spectacle. I have already said that mechanical things are a closed book to me. In New York everything was mechanical, and I had to get used to the fact and adapt myself to it.

The warmth of the American welcome is not a myth: like all foreigners, I benefited from it and derived a great deal of pleasure from it, as warmth and friendship are two things I cannot live without. I quickly made the acquaintance of Mme Engel, who, at the request of mutual friends, was delighted to take me in charge and serve as my mentor. Later she was to play an extremely important role in the life of Maison Christian Dior – New York. I also met Edward Marcus, one of the associates of the firm which had been responsible for my invitation, and who had been sent to meet me; both he and his wife became good friends of mine.

Finally, I set off for Dallas. I had no idea what to expect of a town which answered to such a romantic name. In fact Dallas is a massive block of skyscrapers, grouped round a square so that the church, the town hall, the school, and the hotel were situated exactly like the same institutions in a French village, except that the height of everything was multiplied twenty or thirty times. These skyscrapers are occupied by banks and offices of all sorts (naturally there are numerous petrol companies). They are surrounded by residential districts of charming houses built in a familiar architectural style, separated one from the other by stretches of green lawn and well-cared-for gardens.

But when one examines the structure of Dallas seriously, one realizes that its real singularity consists in the fact that it is constructed around a smart shop, one of the most luxurious in the whole of the United States. This extraordinary establishment, which owes its foundation to the genius of the family of Neiman Marcus, offers the most expensive things in the world to the richest people in the world. European readers may perhaps be surprised to learn that this one Neiman Marcus shop is enough to make Dallas famous in the four corners of the United States. In France something parallel occurs, when a tiny village achieves fame through one gastronomic speciality.

I did not arrive in Dallas alone. I had a French mentor with me, André Janet, who had lived many years in America. His task was to smooth both my journey and my stay in Dallas. First of all he told me that the celebrated Hollywood dress designer, Irene, and the famous Italian shoemaker, Salvatore Ferragamo, would be receiving Oscars at the same time as me. The idea of this 'trades union' of Oscar-winners did something to calm my apprehension. But Janet then proceeded to double my fears by telling me that I would receive the prize on a golden platform in front of three thousand people. It would be a silver plaque mounted on ebony, which was to be awarded to me for my services in the field of fashion, and, horrors, I would then have to make a short speech in English! It was extremely hot in Dallas, but when I heard this news I went cold all over.

That night I slept very badly. The next day, amongst other novelties, I discovered for the first time what in fact turned out to be my daily menu during the course of my tour: piles of sandwiches, cold turkey, and iced ham cooked in sugar in the Virginian fashion – which luckily I happen to like very much – the whole meal gulped down while standing up, and washed down with orangeade, since there was no hope of a glass of wine, and I detest both iced water and iced milk.

At nine o'clock in the evening after a giddy round of cocktail parties I finally found myself sitting down, but alas on the famous gilded platform, facing the aforesaid three thousand spectators. The central hall of the Marcus shop was entirely hung with golden lamé and transformed into a garden of the Hesperides by a forest of orange trees, hung with their own fruit. As the orchestra struck up, model girls wearing my dresses started to file past. By the end of the afternoon, I was worn out trying to convince my questioners that the principal attraction and novelty of the evening dresses consisted in the well-displayed bosom: Marilyn Monroe had not yet been launched and everyone looked at me as if I had committed a terrible error of taste.

By now the fatal moment of the presentation of the Oscar was almost upon me. My co-laureates had already been honoured: I had been saved up till last, as a particularly choice victim. Suddenly, just as M. Ferragamo was receiving his silver plaque, my terror gave place to inspiration. What was I making all the fuss about – I, a Parisian *couturier* abroad, who would be expected to cut an eccentric figure in any case? Having always enjoyed a game of charades, I decided that this evening I was going to impersonate a certain character called Christian Dior, a *couturier* who couldn't speak a word of English and had to stumble out a speech in the language. The room burst into roars of laughter, and with relief I descended from the platform. I had not disappointed my public, and my theatrical verve lasted me throughout my tour of the United States.

I left Dallas with many feelings of regret. The Marcus family had managed to transform an official visit into an unofficial, friendly one by their great personal kindness to me. It is one of the most praiseworthy American characteristics, to be able to pass naturally from the realm of business contacts to that of delightful warm-hearted *camaraderie*.

I now prepared myself to enter a considerably more familiar world – California – the earthly paradise of which all Americans, and many Europeans, dream. I expected a perpetually warm climate, a perpetually shining sun, a profusion of trees, flowers, and wide sandy beaches, washed by the last waves of the Pacific breakers – in fact, a super Riviera. I also prepared myself for Los Angeles with its film stars, and Beverly Hills with its dream-like luxury. To this mental picture I added the vivid Mediterranean colouring of Cannes and Portofino. However on my way to this artificial Eden, Arizona intervened with all its savage reality, which defied anything I had imagined: grandiose canyons, mountains of the moon, petrified forests … It reminded me of the pictures of Salvador Dalí: there were the same ranges of cliffs, painted by the sun in every colour in the prism, and looking like frozen rainbows.

After this interval of inspired tourism, Los Angeles and the Pacific coast were the complete opposite of what I had expected. The ocean was white and grey, not blue, with hideous villages of corrugated iron or wood, chains of petrol pumps and ugly villas all along its shores. As for Los Angeles, so charmingly named, I can honestly say that it would be impossible for any Frenchman used to logically constructed buildings and towns built according to some sort of plan, not to be appalled by the untidy appearance of this enormous agglomeration of buildings, occupying 500 square miles.

But if Los Angeles was not what Christian Dior had been expecting, Los Angeles had certainly been expecting Christian Dior – for a Press conference, endless visits to shops, lethal cocktails, fork lunches, fashion shows, and even a shower of anonymous letters, written by the enemies of the 'liberated bosom', of rounded hips, of long skirts, in short of the New Look. Unperturbed, I faced a battery of flash bulbs, I smiled, shook hands, drank orangeade, and increased my self-confidence in the role which I had recently created for myself in Dallas.

By contrast I found Beverly Hills more peaceful than I had hoped. The film stars were mostly away on holiday, and the town was peaceful. Charming hosts, some of whom had been recommended to me by Lady Mendl, gave me a series of warm welcomes in delightful houses. I met René Clair and his wife Brognia again, and found they had brought all the atmosphere of distant France with them; I discovered real friends – a rare piece of good luck – in the Groves and Jane Magnin. I was taken to see the film studios of 20th Century Fox. When I left this factory of illusions, I personally had none left, and I thanked my lucky stars that I earned my living in the more solid sphere of fashion. But if Los Angeles was not to my taste, the Californian countryside delighted me. Stretches of green velvet embroidered with orange trees and lemon trees – it had all the luxuriance of Normandy and the Campanie seen in the clear light of the Côte Basque.

The West Coast Americans seem to me to be like the Swiss and divide into two camps. In Switzerland there are the fans of Basel and the fans of Zürich: the Americans divide into the San Franciscans and the Los Angelists. Let me say at once that I am a San Franciscan. This city, whose hills are scattered with houses painted pink, pale green, and yellow, which is flanked on three sides by water, and has thrown across its bay the dizziest of bridges, offers in a single bouquet the charms of Naples, Istanbul, China, and Luna Park fun-fair. It owes this last characteristic to its streets, sheer precipices with a gradient of 1 in 3, which have steps as pavements and funiculars as tramways. Cars ascend or descend them like sledges on the Russian mountains. Did I say that it is its Luna Park aspect which I liked best of all? The scenic railway and the water chute made my childhood a misery, but San Francisco is so beautiful that I finished by even loving the memory of my childish dizziness. Moreover, the temperature there all the year round is 'air conditioned', both fresh and gently moist.

A huge crowd of people greeted me at the aerodrome. I also found a heap of invitations waiting for me, which left me with the horrid problem of trying to please everyone, without offending anyone. I was given the symbolic keys of the town in a golden box at one club, while a number of people waited at another club, annoyed at not seeing me turn up for the same ceremony.

But the easy-going happy Italianate atmosphere of San Francisco made it seem simple to sort the various confusions out. I got through all the functions imposed on me by politeness or commercial good sense, quickly but conscientiously. Then, with a feeling of liberation, I set out to explore the city from top to bottom.

I loved feeling I was Chinese as I wandered through the streets of Chinatown, decked with shop-signs as alluring as they were incomprehensible. The shops revealed strange marvels to me, which should have graced the cupboard of an amateur scientist in the eighteenth century – mermaids, mushrooms, wizards' eggs, shark fins, Mandragora roots – everything for the amateur alchemist! I liked to feel myself Spanish under the pavings of the yellow and green painted churches on the tops of the hills, Neapolitan as I wandered through the dock districts, French at the extreme point of the bay, visiting the Corots and the Nattiers, exhibited in an exact replica of the *hôtel de la Légion d'Honneur*, on the front of which are inscribed the words *'Honneur et Patrie'*.

One other pleasure San Francisco afforded me. I left it with regret because my stay had been so short, but some French friends of mine who visited it later, told me that a whole case in the city's museum of art and history contains a permanent exhibition of several of my models.

From San Francisco I went by train to Chicago. What a train! Its coaches were as comfortable as the apartments of a palace, but as depressing as rooms in a hospital; they also had the irritating quality of being too light in weight, so that they swayed without stopping. As I bumped and jolted through the splendours of the Californian scenery, already familiar to me from gangster films and the novels of Sinclair Lewis, I tried to prepare myself for the monotony of yet another Press conference. Fortunately I had ended by seeing the funny side of these ludicrous cross-examinations, which force you to ponder heavily on actions which were made at the time without any soul-searching; their ingenuous brutality also obliges one to evolve a new form of politeness. The rules of the game are that you have to reply in the sense expected by your interviewers, without being rude. At the slightest sign of difficulty, you change the subject. The art lies in managing to be amusing at the same time either by what one says, or by one's behaviour.

The questions are the same the world over. They ask you:

'Are the women here the most beautiful in the world?' I invariably reply that French women aren't at all bad either.

'What is the right length for a skirt? What will be the trend of your next collection?'

To the last question I generally reply very innocently that I haven't the least idea – which is generally true – and even if it isn't, it gives me an excellent excuse for keeping silent.

In the train which bore me towards Chicago, I recapitulated my jokes and practised my expressions and gestures. Thus prepared, I awaited the entry to the station without a great deal of anxiety. Imagine how surprised I was to see the same anxiety from which I had just been liberated stamped on the faces of those about to interview me. They hustled me towards the waiting cars. It was only when the doors were closed that my guards gave a sigh of relief, as if we had all escaped arrest. They then explained to me that because the train had been late, I had to dress in a hurry in order to go to the inevitable fashion show, which had already begun.

As the Americans, contrary to their reputation, are in fact the most leisured people in the world, I was at a loss to understand this mad haste. It was only when I arrived at the reception that I understood. The hall – as no doubt the station had been too – was patrolled in every sense of the word by suffragette housewives brandishing placards on sticks, bearing the words:

'Down With the New Look', 'Burn Monsieur Dior', 'Christian Dior, Go Home.'

In order to escape these Maenads, I, the new Orpheus, had somehow to pass through them unobserved. My guard of honour wanted to disguise me: but their precautions were needless. My own phlegmatic appearance was the best possible protection. I do not know what sort of mental image they had formed of the hated Dior – they were probably on the look-out for a pin-up boy. At any rate, I passed through the hall without question, and my solid Norman looks aroused not the faintest breath of curiosity. All the same, I was a little disappointed!

I was able to wander about Chicago quite freely, when I had some free time, certain that I would not be recognized. At the risk of disappointing New York or Boston intellectuals and the majority of Europeans who visit the U.S., I will openly admit my taste for this strange energetic city of contrasts, where the most outrageous luxury exists side by side with the most disturbing poverty. Once past its superb rampart of palaces, skyscrapers, banks, private houses raised up on the shores of Lake Michigan, one discovers the true face of Chicago. It is the only American city which really resembles the films or novels which it has inspired. The iron staircases running down the faces of buildings, the viaducts, the neon signs of all colours, the dusty windows, the heterogeneous crowd in the streets, from Greeks and Poles to Letts and Hungarians – above all, the thin veil of ash, which the chimneys of the canned-meat factories puff out over everything – this is America in the raw, the most authentic expression of the spirit of the country.

Chicago, in spite of its ominous reputation, is one of the most poetic cities in the world. Among other things, it possesses a museum where one can admire the best collection of Impressionist pictures in the world, masterpieces which it is sad for a Frenchman to see exiled, as it were, from the land where they were painted. The lack of initiative of our own museums combined with the cupidity of picture dealers and the lack of appreciation of the public, have resulted in our being obliged to admire them far from their native land.

Washington, city of diplomats, followed the city of gangsters. How could I fail to admire this city whose *Versaillaise* vistas are in fact the work of a Frenchman? European and American visitors generally concur in finding the Washington atmosphere stiff and forbidding. Personally, owing to the great kindness of the French Ambassador there, M. Bonnet, and Mme Bonnet, I found a welcome which was anything but cold. It is always amusing for the irreverent to observe the diplomatic world. Among other things, I greatly appreciated the personality of those famous Washington hostesses, whose receptions fill the gossip columns the length of the U.S.A. These ladies, who both physically and mentally are on a grand scale, are real queens, in a country which still rather charmingly prides itself on being the most democratic of republics.

From Washington's marble Palladian porticos to the painted wooden porticos of Boston and Massachusetts: it is wonderful to cross New England, the most ancient and deeply civilized part of America. In Boston I found again that English way of life which I love, and spent a great deal of time in the remarkable museums and universities. French students, condemned to haunt our own deliberately austere faculties, would find it difficult to imagine their comfort and beauty.

Finally, I returned to New York, the beginning and end of my journey. At the start, I had only passed through it, and knew no more of the city than the average American who drives smartly through Paris knows of it. I enjoyed looking up many of my old friends, who had landed up there during the war, and decided to make it their home. They taught me to know, understand, and love New York, the city to which I have since returned twenty times, and which is now almost as much home to me as Paris.

The first discovery I made was that New York – one of the great capitals of the world – is in fact nothing but a village. It is also a village with strict geographical limits consisting of twenty streets, within which there are five hotels, three restaurants, and four night-clubs. There, and there only, will you find the three hundred people who make up New York. And as the problem of going any way by car has become insoluble, you will meet them every day, strolling along the pavement, exactly as one parades along the boulevards in Paris. If you stray far from Fifth Avenue and Park Avenue, you leave the village. You risk losing yourself immediately in Harlem, in Downtown, or on the West Side, the district where nobody is supposed to live, which is a pity, as it contains some very pretty houses. Of course there is absolutely no question of living in Brooklyn: it seems much further away than Connecticut or Long Island, which are actually far more distant but are admissible residential areas for Café Society.

Café Society in New York is as exclusive as an English club. Its members frequent the five hotels, the three restaurants, and the four nightclubs already mentioned. They only meet each other and never go outside the three territories which are limited by, on one side Fifth Avenue and the East River, and on the other, approximately by 45th and 50th Streets. These frontiers are in fact so precisely defined that I apologize if I have in fact given them inaccurately, having no memory for numbers. More strictly enclosed within its boundaries than the Emperor of China in his Forbidden City or the Pope in the Vatican, Café Society lives in the shadow of its skyscrapers as French villagers live in the shadow of the trees of their market square. The financier can go every day to Wall Street; the smart women can depart every weekend for Long Island or go to Europe, but their private life cannot be lived anywhere else except within these sacred limits. The result of this fidelity is that one always finds the same faces in the same places. You get used to them, and they get used to you, and you soon have the agreeable sensation of having been accepted by them.

In spite of this delightful contact with Café Society, I pushed my investigations further into the American way of life, knowledge of which I consider indispensable for every denizen of the twentieth century. As my stay reached its end I felt increasingly a confused but nevertheless tenacious desire to return to New York some day, to achieve something there and win a place for myself in this Eldorado. Mixed with this feeling was the vague wish – common to many Europeans in 1947 – to plant one foot in America, while keeping the other in the Old World. With time I have discovered that it would be impossible for me to live permanently far from my own country, but as a contrast, the pleasure of revisiting New York remains always as great as ever.

The French often picture New York as a conglomeration of sky-scrapers and streets meeting at right angles. In truth the geometry of the town is of infinite variety, but consists of geometry in space. It does not exist in plan but in volume. The most striking feature of the city is the juxtaposition of infinitely tall houses with those which are infinitely small – of luxurious quarters with slums. This juxta-position, which does not seem to worry anybody, is effected with no feeling of transition. My passion for antique furniture took me into the antique district, and then I wanted to explore Greenwich Village, which plays the role in New York of Montmartre and Montparnasse in Paris. Strolling about the streets often took me to the West Side, and one Sunday morning I even reached Wall Street, a great silent and deserted nave, floating in the Sabbath calm like a stranded cathedral. As taxis in New York can only be taken by storm, one goes further on foot there than in any other city in the world.

Now I come to the question which I have been asked a thou-sand times, and I know perfectly well my readers are waiting for me to answer:

'What do you think of American women?'

My answer will probably both surprise and disappoint you. The blonde and willowy women whom Hollywood delights to exhibit to us I find not in any way essentially different from their European sisters. When André Siegfried returned to New York after the war, he was amazed to no longer find the monumental, cumbersome, actress-type American beauty, which he had found at the end of the preceding century. 'The American female has changed her physical type since then,' he concluded. In fact in 1947 there existed one essential difference between the women of the Old World and the New, which has been greatly reduced since. In 1947 American women had all the shiny brilliance of a new penny. Their clothes were impeccable, their hair and their nails were impeccable, their shoes were impeccable. In short, the Americans were impeccable. It was true of all classes of society from the millionaires down to the liftman's daughter.

If I would have had my compatriots emulate some of this impeccability, I must at the same time admit that in the end all this perfection gave an impression of uniformity. However, in order to struggle against it, all the resources of a rich and variegated collection of ready-made clothes were mobilized with, very often, regrettable lack of discernment. A hat bought here, a coat there, a dress somewhere else – pretty enough in themselves – made up an outfit perhaps, but not an *ensemble*. I realized that the clear vibrant air of New York justifies in some part these bold essays of colour which started on the paintwork of the cars, continued on to the dresses of the passengers, or the hideous ties of the drivers, and all appeared to be battling against each other. A certain taste for exaggeration nullifies the American elegance.

But times have changed. America has renounced its excesses just as France has renounced its *zazou* follies. For its part, France has been able to dress itself with more care, and benefit from a greater variety of clothing at its disposal. America has had its influence on Europe and vice versa; these two quarters of the world are too much sisters under the skin for them to be able to endure separation for long without harm. So, with the years, the face of New York has changed. The taste for subtle colours, the smartest of all tastes, has developed.

What alarmed me most in the course of my stay in the United States was the habit of spending enormous sums of money in order to achieve so little real luxury. America – thus realizing the idea of Soviet Russia – represents the triumph of the quantitative over the qualitative. Men and women both prefer buying a multitude of mediocre things to acquiring a few carefully chosen articles. The American woman, faithful to the ideal of optimism which the United States seem to have made their rule of life, seems to spend money entirely in order to gratify the collective need to buy. She prefers three new dresses to one beautiful one. She never hangs back from making a choice, knowing perfectly well that her fancy will be of short duration and the dress which she is in the process of buying will be jettisoned very soon.

In spite of all this, the women of New York are marvellously protected against errors of taste. Their shops offer them the pick of the world's fashions; the *boutiques* offer them the complete run of the creations of every country. In spite of that, we still say in Europe that they do not know how to buy. We are in the habit of buying something because we think it beautiful or of good workmanship, and we consider the use we will put it to, as much as its appearance. Can one therefore conclude that abundance risks blunting taste? Poverty is an astonishing magic wand. A woman who can only afford to buy one dress, generally goes to such trouble to choose it that she makes a good buy. She very often achieves more elegance than the woman who possesses several.

These reflections on America do not bring me to any pessimistic conclusion. We live in the times we do; and nothing is sillier than to turn one's back on them. It is therefore without bitterness that I state that this famous Café Society, where I have known so many charming friends, represents in America no more than a tiny minority, which is in process of disappearing. Millionaires of the old sort are becoming as rare as the last Indians. Nothing now distinguishes them from the well-to-do worker; both appreciate the average mechanical comfort, which today is tending to replace luxury.

Paris, on the other hand, represents the sense of finish and perfection. It is there, more than anywhere else, that quality of craftsmanship is really understood and we Frenchmen must preserve this tradition. My knowledge of America helped me to understand France and its resources better, and filled me with a strong desire to return home. I had just been plunged into the most complete expression of the twentieth century functional; now I was longing, in spite of the glories and grandeurs of New York, for the sense of proportion of ancient Europe.

It had been wonderful experiencing the American way of life for several weeks, and adopting habits which I would have to be careful to drop the moment I returned to France. There an altogether different mode of life, more old-fashioned, but better suited to my nature, was waiting for me. When I arrived back, I could have kissed the earth, and taken off my hat to every blade of grass, I was so happy.

An extraordinary emotion transfixes me every time I return home. I pity those who are not sufficiently attached to a particular civilization to experience this feeling. The most humble landscapes seem to me to be bathed in a special light because they are part of my home. These stones which have been coated with the patina of time, are my own stones. Even the carelessness which I detect, is the carelessness of my own country, and has its charm for me.

When I got back, Paris had still not forgotten the war. The wounds in its walls were still there. But above the city floated the clear blue sky of the Île-de-France – my beloved and incomparable sky.

PART TWO

FROM THE IDEA TO THE DRESS

— 5 —

THE IDEA

At the risk of being thought soulless, and in spite of my love of architecture and interior decoration, I must admit that clothes are my whole life. Ultimately everything I know, see, or hear, every part of my life, turns around the clothes which I create. They haunt me perpetually, until they are ready to pass from the world of my dreams into the world of practical utility.

How then is a collection created? I am often asked where I get my inspiration from: but I can honestly say that I do not know. Perhaps a psychoanalyst – who was also a dress designer – would be able to make some useful observations on the subject by comparing my successive collections with my emotions at various stages in my past life. But he would not have the mass of documents which people fondly imagine that the *couturier* searches through for inspiration, to help him. I do not say that there is necessarily anything wrong with this method of designing, but I do say that it has never been of any help to me. Far from stimulating me, an exact historical source in front of me curtails my imagination. A particular country, style, or epoch are only interesting for the ideas behind them; looking at an old design might incline one to copy it without fresh inspiration. This is so true that, even when I am designing the costumes for an historical play, I firmly shut my books, once I have consulted them, put away my prints, and allow a certain amount of time to elapse before taking up my pencil. That is the only real way one can recreate in the spirit of the century where the action is supposed to take place. An exhibition or a museum are important sources of inspiration, chiefly with regard to details.

Fashion has a life and laws of its own which are difficult for the ordinary intelligence to grasp. Personally, I know exactly what I must give to my designs: care, trouble, and enthusiasm. They must be the reflection of my everyday existence, showing the same feelings, the same joys, the same tenderness.

The most passionate adventures of my life have therefore been with my clothes. I am obsessed with them. They preoccupy me, they occupy me, and finally they 'post-occupy' me, if I can risk the word. This half vicious, half ecstatic circle, makes my life at the same time heaven and hell.

The prime need of fashion is to please and attract, consequently this attraction must never result in uniformity, the mother of boredom. That is why, although there is no logic in the development of fashion, it has a kind of logical sensitivity which obeys one or two reflexes: reaction or confirmation.

By the end of October, after three months of intensive study, I have separated 'that which I still love' from 'that which I no longer love', and am progressing rapidly towards 'that which I shall love in the future'. For my seasonal love affair with fashion begins on the very morning when my last collection was presented to the public.

Hidden behind the grey satin curtain which divides me from the *salon*, I listen eagerly to the greeting accorded to the first showing of my dresses: for this is the moment of their true debut. Like certain women, they only spring to life when they are admired. That is why I cross-examine the mannequins anxiously about the effect produced by certain models which I consider particularly important. I open my ears wide to the opinions of others: my friends, my clients, the journalists, and the professional buyers – they all contribute something of value to the new fashion which is conceived in the confusion of congratulations which follows the first official showing of my previous collection. One's sensitivity is acute and one notices the least nuance in the reception of each model. One experiences tremendous pleasure from the triumph of one model, a pang from the semi-failure, or just-not-success of another. Of course, the slightest criticism murmured in between two sips of champagne can arouse a burning fire in my breast. Curiously enough, in the great ball of the collection it is sometimes the beloved models, the favourite children, which are unjustly wallflowers: so that even in the sweetness of success there is some drop of bitterness and disappointment.

A historian like my friend Gaxotte reckons that fifty years have to elapse before one can give a considered opinion on any event: but I never have more than three months in which to reflect on my past collection, before I have to return to work. 'Fashion dies young,' wrote Cocteau, and it is therefore natural that its rhythm should be more hectic than that of history.

The weeks which follow the first showing have a decisive influence on the collection which is yet to be born. It is then that I perform my ritual self-criticism, in which I am assisted by the photographs or drawings published in the papers which often present me with an entirely new light on my creations. A detail which I had inserted without thinking, and which had become lost in the course of the execution of the dress, will emerge miraculously under the pencil of the artist or through the objective lens of the camera, as a result of a curious angle or unexpected lighting. Perhaps these revelations are a proof of the independence of my creations from their creator.

Even more useful to me is seeing my dresses live upon the backs of my clients. Although I very rarely go into the fitting room, I have all its echoes sedulously reported to me. Thus I am kept fully informed about the choice of the professional buyers and those of my privileged clients who do not always agree with my judgement. Supplemented by other reports from the workrooms, these reports weave a sort of net on which I have to embroider the theme of the next collection. For all this time I am meeting my dresses again. Like dear friends, I meet them all the time at dinners and balls; a little later I meet them in the street – already getting further away from the original, because they are copies. Finally I discover them, major or minor travesties of my original conception, in the windows of the shops. But even the copies, even the adaptations which are more like deformations, are of use to me; in terms of a certain saturation, they show me all the pitfalls into which I have fallen, which gives me both a shock and a lesson. Every woman invests a dress with her particular personality; thus a model worn by Marie looks quite different when Chantale wears it; one extinguishes but the other transfigures it. Having decided on the difference, I still have to analyse the reason for it.

That terrible calculating, professional's eye which I apparently possess – I suppose I shall never lose it. I have been told that women feel undressed beneath my stern regard! They are wrong: I am simply redressing them in quite different clothes. But even this harmless intention must shine out of my eyes, for it embarrasses the lady I am speaking to, and also gives me a complex once I discover what is happening. But I apply it to all women, to close friends as to a strange woman I see coming into the room for the first time. Incidentally, my professional's eye also inhibits me from paying a compliment to a pretty woman wearing one of my dresses, because I might seem to be attributing to myself part of her success; this discretion has its advantages, because if it imposes silence upon me when I am satisfied, it also allows me to keep silence when I am disappointed. I have sworn to mention no individual names here because it would be unbecoming to turn this book into a sort of *Concours d'Élégance*, but I should just like to take the opportunity to express my profound gratitude to all the women who have given me so much pleasure by understanding how to wear my dresses.

If I worry about the way my dresses are worn out in the world, I worry equally about those of my rivals, which teach me how they have disposed of the same problems which face me. It is strange and impalpable – this influence which the *couturiers* have on each other. It arises from the fact that every season there exist, spread among the various *couture* houses, two or three pilot models created either by chance or by deliberate choice, which will determine the trend of the future. Meanwhile, the need for synthesis makes the newspapers impose an artificial unity upon the season's fashions. The apparently prevailing trend is the choice of the journalists and the clients. The exigencies of distribution and the modern taste for slogans, accentuate this simplification still further and induce all women to buy more or less the same dress. In this way each collection contains about twenty dresses, which become the 'best-sellers'.

In their shadow the pilot models of which I have spoken often pass unappreciated. But the famous professional eye is not mistaken; every *couturier* takes advantage of it in order to pick up a lesson from a rival, or to decide to put an end to the diffusion of a certain fashion (often after several seasons), thus condemning it to vulgarization and finally to disappearance. One can only say that these are the models which truly mould fashion and distil that unique air of Paris which is so often praised. Otherwise sobriety of elegance and rare rightness of taste are surely not enough to explain why so many collections – each one hugging its secrets tight – disclose the same magic formula on the appointed day.

The mid-season collections formerly marked the passing of the purely critical period into the period of creation. Three months after the major collection the big houses produced a remoulded and refashioned version of it – a sort of 'digest' of its ideas. These mid-season collections were intended to reawaken the interest of the *clientèle* by introducing about thirty new models, certain of which accentuated the principal tendencies of the big collection, while others paved the way for something new. But as the seasons grew longer and specialized hand labour rarer, this type of collection more or less died out.

That is why I always get so much satisfaction from designing the collection which I do for my New York house. It fulfils the same function in my mind as the mid-season collections did before the war. Proceeding from a theme which is familiar to me and which only recently has completely absorbed my energies, I effect revisions and transformations. Some of the models have to be adapted to the needs of the American wholesalers, that is to say, to the needs of a much larger public. Ordinarily I start by introducing certain simplifications, but if one works in the grip of an inspiration which one has already fully experienced, sooner or later one is bound to look out for new and different elements to incorporate. One gets bored with recopying. That is how a transitional style is gradually effected. The New York collection is far from being a mere reproduction of the Paris collection; nearly always several models in it presage the major trend of tomorrow's collection. But before designing this, I allow myself a whole month of meditation and mental exploration.

One of the strangest facts about the *couturier*'s profession – which the uninitiated find most incomprehensible – is that a fashion is always decided *out* of season. The winter collection is worked upon in the season of lilac and cherry-blossom, the summer collection when the leaves or the first snow is falling. We *couturiers* are like poets. A little nostalgia is necessary for us. We like to dream of summer in the middle of winter and vice versa. It would be as impossible for me to create a summer dress in the month of August as it would be to create a new model outside the context of the whole collection. Equally indispensable for the creator are the distance which separates him from the season for which he is designing and the infinite variety of the completed collection.

Back to the actual creation of my collection: during the first days of the rest which I allow myself, tortured by regret, caprice, and curiosity all at once, I abstain from designing altogether. I am frightened of giving birth to premature designs whose insufficiently developed forms will encumber me in the future. Half irritated, half happy at what I have already decided, above all longing to put my thoughts down on paper, I spend several weeks in this state of gestation. Finally I retire to the country. This migration resembles the journey of the eels to the Sargasso Sea, or the gathering of penguins on their island. When I set off, I already know that between the first and the fifteenth of the month I shall have covered endless blocks of paper with a crowd of tiny hieroglyphical figures, which I alone can decipher.

I scribble everywhere, in bed, in my bath, at meals, in my car, on foot, in the sun, in electric light, by day, and by night. Bed and bath, where one is not conscious, so to speak, of one's body, are particularly favourable to inspiration; here one's spirit is at ease. There is also the element of chance inspiration – stones, trees, human beings, mere gestures, or a sudden ray of light, may be bearers of little whispered messages. As Leonardo da Vinci walked in the Florentine countryside, he observed the patterns in the sand or the sky and transposed them into his pictures in the forms of patches of light. On a more modest scale, my dresses take shape all around me, as my fancy works on whatever it happens to see.

Suddenly one such flash of inspiration gives me an electric shock. I am possessed, and embroider endless variations on this one theme. The next morning it is the turn of another line – which has perhaps come to me during the night – to give me the signal. The design seems to hail you like a friend encountering you in the street when you are on holiday. You tell yourself that there can be no doubt about it at all – it *is* your friend. As you run to meet her, you feel a sense of conspiracy between you, based on the fact that you have always known her. On the whole, the models which are created after such flashes of inspiration are the most successful ones of all.

Little by little, the pile of drawings grows, demanding new treatments capable of exploring all their potentialities. Finally this crazy burst of scribbling comes to an end. Then I behave like a baker who knows when to leave a well-kneaded pastry alone. Now that the line from which the new fashion can emerge is determined, I stop. For several days I put aside all thoughts connected with fashion. The revision which follows this interlude gains sureness from the rest which I have had. I examine all my sketches, from the first, which are scarcely more than rough outlines, to the last born, where the shape is much more clearly defined. The selection takes place more or less automatically. I sense from the first what promises well; the worthless element eliminates itself. Next, within the space of two or three days, I execute several hundred designs in order to give my ideas a practical expression. Ideas flock into my head one after the other; a single sketch starts off a whole series. The sum of these drawings constitutes the base of the future collection: and now I am in haste to get them to the workrooms, in order that the sketches shall be transformed into dresses.

Up till now I have only discussed the actual designing of dresses. When it comes to giving them a practical expression, it is time for the thousand hands who fashion, cut, baste, and mount a dress to intervene. From my corps of helpers in the studio, down to the youngest apprentices, the avenue Montaigne becomes a hive of industry. For now I put my sketches, piping hot, into the hands of Mme Marguerite.

I seat myself at a light table near the window of the studio, surrounded by Mme Marguerite, Mme Raymonde, and Mme Bricart. Suddenly a doubt strikes me. The optics of the studio are different from those of the places where I have been designing: they recreate immediately an atmosphere of work, of exigency even. How will my designs, which I think now are so familiar to me, strike me in this new light? Designs can be clumsy or precise. They depend on good luck with one's draftsmanship, and one's mood at the moment of creation; the important thing about them is that they should be expressive. The great mistake of the fashion schools is teaching their pupils simply to turn out finished drawings or abstract patterns. In order to excite the enthusiasm of a *première* – or mine, for that matter – a sketch must suggest both attack and allure; it must already suggest a living line; it must be redolent with movement.

My preliminary sketches, which in the charming if archaic language of *couture*, are still called *'petites gravures'*, have been simply scrawled down, and do not give the details of a *toilette*, unless it incorporates some striking new feature. As they are passed from hand to hand, I comment on them and fill in the picture with the help of a few purely technical explanations, about the cut, or the lay of the material. This is the first step in the metamorphosis of the sketch into the dress. I survey the sketch again in the light of the reactions of my faithful counsellors. As the designs accumulate, a certain tendency becomes noticeable. One halts suddenly in front of one of them and exclaims:

'Oh, I love that one!'

It is passed round from hand to hand, its details are carefully studied; then we all turn back to the sketches which went before it. Thanks to the impression which the last sketch made upon us, the others now take on a new significance. In the majority of cases these revelations after the event teach us the same lesson: it is the simplest line, the most self-explanatory design – where the principle of the dress is most clearly stated – which wins us over. It conquers us because its very simplicity exudes vitality. Over and over again in the course of our studies the word 'expression' occurs:

'Have I expressed you correctly?' Marguerite asks me. I tell the *première*, 'Your dress has not got the expression I want!' For the art of making a dress from a design lies in achieving the correct 'expression'.

Some people have done me the honour of finding in each of my successive collections a *signification d'ensemble*. In all humility I am prepared to believe they are right. Although the *couturier* is naturally anxious to sew and cut well, he feels all the time this desire to express himself. For all its ephemerality, *couture* constitutes a mode of self-expression which can be compared to architecture or painting.

Once I have shown all my sketches, Mme Marguerite distributes the *'petites gravures'* according to personal preferences. The *premiers* and *premières* are allowed a certain liberty of choice, for after all one can only 'express' with justice that which one feels with one's heart.

As Mme Marguerite distributes the designs, she recapitulates and develops the points which I have made to her. If I happen to come into the studio when she is in the midst of her explanations, I am touched to see the interest and enthusiasm on the faces round me. Everybody seems to be anxious to grasp the problems posed by the new designs: and in their anxiety not to let the least detail escape them, even the most experienced of the *premières* shows the eagerness and freshness of a beginner.

Like sap, the creative idea circulates now throughout the whole building. It reaches the apprentices and the seamstresses, and inspires the fingers which are working on the *toiles* – in short, the fingers which are fashioning the styles of tomorrow. For one week the house is a busy hive of questions and cross-questions.

Everyone works out his own solution to the problem of the new line and compares it with that evolved by a neighbouring worker. I resolutely refuse to interfere in this process. I believe that each of my workers should be left free to work out his or her form of self-expression, because I take into account the possibility of some new technical discovery in the course of such experiments.

The *première* examines her appointed sketch, pulls it to pieces, takes it away with her, gets the feel of it, and finally drapes her *toile* around a dummy figure. Then she steps back, examines the effect, corrects it, balances it, and often entirely destroys it in order to start again. After several fruitless attempts, the exact meaning of the material becomes apparent to her and the dress starts to take shape. An assistant is then called to pin the *toile*, which is still only draped. Little by little the pile of sketches diminishes in each workroom as the models are divided up among the most competent hands.

I bite my nails and, in order to have something to do, I choose the buttons, the belts, the accessories, and the jewels to be worn with each dress. I also choose materials from rolls which have been ordered several weeks before, an almost ritual ceremony which I will describe later. During the week when I am waiting for the *toiles* to make their first appearance, I involve myself in these various activities more for the sake of calming my nerves than for getting on with the work.

— 6 —

FROM THE 'TOILE' TO THE DRESS

The new collection is like the arrival of spring in the studio. During the off season it is as white, empty, and gloomy as a laboratory; now the pieces of material are like young shoots which ripen into a thousand flowery patterns.

Belts hang in dozens from the tables; scarves and hats clutter up the shelf under the blackboard where the names of the mannequins are written. In every direction, there are signs that the new collection is being prepared. This happy world of wool and silk is sternly guarded against intruders. Whenever there is a rumour that a stranger is approaching, veils of white *toile* are flung over everything, covering the new materials and obscuring the accessories. The busy workroom is transformed in an instant into a peaceful deserted *salon*. This little comedy never ceases to amuse me.

When the veils are removed, the studio is once again a hive of life and the great day approaches when the first *toiles* are to be shown. Of course Mme Marguerite turns faint at the idea of showing them to me, and the *premières* are terrified that they have made some awful mistake. Even I myself begin to wonder what these dream-children of mine will really look like when I am actually confronted with them.

What follows next is a solemn moment for us all. The first *toiles* generally number about sixty, and they consist of reproductions of the most significant of the '*petites gravures*'; those which I have asked to see at once. Now at last I do see them!

Two or three of my mannequins are chosen to show them to me. Of course all the '*jeunes filles*' (as we call the mannequins) who work for me are both graceful and pretty, but inevitably certain of them inspire me more than others. Undoubtedly there exists between these girls and me a kind of sympathy or sense of affinity, which I imagine obeys the usual mechanical rules which govern these attractions. For one must distinguish between the successful and the 'inspiring' mannequin: they are not at all the same thing, since I see my collection with quite different eyes from the general public. The successful mannequin is an extrovert; she carries the practice of the model very far, she has to *'empoigner'* and, in trade jargon, *'enlever'* the dress. The inspiring mannequin, on the other hand, is turned inwards and for me alone expresses the mood, tradition, and line of a dress, from the first hours of its creation.

The *couturier* is too often pictured gaily disposing the folds of a drape upon a mannequin; this happens in fact extremely rarely. One only builds a model after long hours of preliminary labour and then it is constructed on a well-planned base. The process of draping the dress on the mannequin cannot take place until all the cutting of the collection has been satisfactorily accomplished.

The first showing of the *toiles* on the mannequins is done amidst 'Ohs' and 'Ahs', equally expressive of joy and disapproval. Some of the exclamations are more explicit:

'Darling, your *toilette is* perfect!'

'My dear, for heaven's sake throw that dress in the wastepaper basket!'

When a *toile is* successful, one personalizes it immediately; if it is a failure, it is just 'that dress' – impersonal and contemptuous phrase.

Very often the models which captivate us now have been made from sketches which passed under our noses quite unnoticed; now, on the basis of this new inspiration, we build a whole new series of dresses. On the other hand other sketches, which apparently promised great things, only produce *'navets'*, which are speedily eliminated. Some of the *toiles* turn out quite differently from what I had imagined; they are not necessarily failures, but the design has been misinterpreted in some way. The *premières*, like the photographers and fashion artists later, have read into the design some project which I had not intended. An artistic creation, which depends on another brain for its interpretation, often produces some surprises for its author. This applies to dresses as much as to plays. It is up to the designer to know how to reap the best advantages from it.

Therefore, if the outcome is satisfactory, I let the model go forward, unless I decide to return to my original project, explaining the design further, or handing it over to a more skilful workroom. Sometimes I entrust the same sketch to several different workrooms, conscious that I will thus obtain the greatest variety of expression in my *toiles*, from which I can either choose the most successful version, or use the variety as a pretext for new departures.

Like the sketches which inspired them, these *toiles* have very little detail; their importance is entirely in their cut, line, and shape. These are the fundamental *toiles* on which the whole collection is based. Details like revers, bows, pockets, or belts, are added later unless they happen to be indispensable to the construction of the model.

The day when the first *toiles* are shown is the crucial day in the whole development of the collection. Now I am able to select from among the models I have designed five or six basic lines, expressed in dresses, costumes, or coats.

Next, I call a grand meeting of my mannequins. I have them all appear in *toilettes* of the same *genre* – all in evening dresses, or all in suits. The session continues until every model has been inspected – often well into the night. As I go home, new designs dance in front of my eyes, and I am in a state of tumult over all I have seen; I am confused and delighted at the same time! I am well aware, of course, that this first moment of enthusiasm will not last: long and hard work lies ahead before these tentative approaches to creation become models worthy of the name.

The next day finds me in a more sober mood, and I decide to see the *toiles* all over again in order to decide which are to be the significant lines of the collection. I have the models paraded before me once more, one by one, in order to have them noted down. The session does not always run absolutely smoothly! Advice is bandied about freely, and a mannequin is sometimes made to show the same dress two or three times, sent out, asked to come in once more … only to find that the model is being tried on another girl. It is fatal to proceed too fast, for one runs the risk of overlooking a basically excellent model, which is temporarily suffering from a mistake in the workmanship. It is only after mature reflection, a hundred questions, and a thousand doubts that a decision is finally taken and duly noted down by Mme Raymonde.

Too often people believe that a collection develops in bursts of enthusiasm and caprice, without any co-ordinated plan. In point of fact, it is always built up along lines which have been established well in advance. Mme Raymonde draws up a complete chart of the collection on several large sheets of paper; she maps out space for a certain number of day dresses, suits, coats, and evening dresses. I force myself to reduce this skeleton plan to the minimum, knowing perfectly well that we shall soon break our bounds. I try to be wary of the seductive pleasures of invention which lure me on towards fresh creations, fully conscious that certain materials and embroideries, which I have already put aside, will oblige me to seek new designs other than those already in existence, to make use of them. I also know that there will always be some last-minute dresses. They are born of various different impulses: in some cases I want to appeal to a type of woman or figure which I have involuntarily neglected; in others I want to underline some detail of the cut or the design which I find to be insufficiently illustrated in the other dresses in the collection.

Even my most fanatical clients and admirers agree that there are always too many models in any one collection. They are absolutely right. A two-hour show without an interval *is* far too long. Besides, it is always too hot in the *salons*. But though it is true that there are far too many dresses for each individual woman, you must not forget that I am addressing myself to a professional *clientèle* – and also clients of vastly differing needs. In every country there are thin women and fat women, dark women and fair women, women of discreet taste, and others whose taste is more flamboyant. There are some women with a beautiful *décolletage*, and others whose aim is to disguise their thighs. Some are too tall. Others are too short. The world is wonderfully full of beautiful women whose shapes and tastes offer an inexhaustible diversity. My collection must cater individually for each one of them, and if I really wanted to satisfy them completely, I should have to design not seventy models but at least seventy times seven. Fortunately, the chart of my collection is there to keep me in check, even though it seems to be acting like a straitjacket on my imagination.

At last the moment has come to decide. The *toiles* which have been judged worthy of transformation into actual models have been classified, described, enumerated, and roughly sketched by Mme Raymonde. Now I have them paraded singly in front of me one last time. The next step is to indicate which mannequin will wear which dress and the material in which it is to be made.

The dress and the mannequin are often as inseparable one from the other as the dress and the material. Of the dozen '*jeunes filles*' who present my collection, three or four of them can put on anything and show it off to advantage. The others probably belong to a more pronounced type of feminine beauty: for them I have to be careful to choose models which will harmonize with their appearance. Not only do I have to consider the physical attributes of my mannequins – I must also be very careful to divide the models equally, else there will be war in the mannequins' *cabine*.

Each girl must show approximately the same number of dresses, and in making up this number, a just balance must be kept between day dresses, elaborate *toilettes* and evening dresses. It is obviously impossible to work this out exactly, and I am frequently made miserable during the show when I see a woollen *tailleur* parade in the midst of a series of more formal dresses, or a short evening dress in the midst of a flow of ball dresses. The most successful model cannot stand up to such unfair competition.

But if the choice of mannequin is important, that of material is even more so because once chosen, it is very hard to remedy a mistake. This very important operation takes place in several stages. Each *couturier* has his own method of work: a few are inspired by the material to create their dresses, but the majority proceed from a *toile* which has been constructed from a sketch or the designer's instructions. Personally, whatever the variety, beauty, or novelty of the stuffs which are displayed to me, they are always a secondary consideration. When work on the new collection is nearing completion, and the new line is finally demarcated in my designs, I do allow myself occasionally to be tempted by the texture, the colour, or the pattern of a particular material. I drape it in folds there and then, as long as I am convinced that there already exists a satisfactory basic design on which the dress can be founded.

My prime inspiration is the shape of the female body: for it is the duty of the *couturier* to adopt the female form as his point of departure and use the materials at his disposal so as to enhance its natural beauty. I have no wish to deprive fashion (and the ladies) of the added allure and charm of colour, but I could perfectly well design a whole collection simply in black or white and express all my ideas to my complete satisfaction. Colour cannot transform a failure of a dress into a success: it merely plays a supporting role in a cast where the cut is the star performer.

In order to relate material to the general background of *haute couture*, I must digress a little. Two months before I have even roughed out my first sketch for the new collection, I have to make my preliminary selection. For that is when they arrive to see me – the silk merchants, the wool merchants, the lace-makers, men of consequence imbued with strong traditions, who come from all over the world, from Paris, London, Lyons, Milan, and Zürich, bringing with them the wealth of the Low Countries and the richness of the Orient.

I await them with my two assistant designers, Mme Raymonde, and my administrative staff at my side. It is like receiving an embassy. Rising to our feet to greet the ambassadors, we solemnly shake hands, and in order not to get on to the subject of the materials piled up in the corridor too quickly, we chat politely about the preceding season. We recall those stuffs which have 'gone well', we give an account of the sales of the models which were made from them, exactly as if we are mutual friends imparting news of other friends whom they have not seen for some time. Then the show starts, and each firm has its characteristic method of display. Some, respectful of the great traditions of the past, are accompanied by a *cortège* of seven or eight trunks which are carried in by bearers, like gifts being brought from far-off countries by Eastern potentates. The head of the firm has them set down, opened, and the carrier spills out the multi-coloured pieces with the quickness of a conjurer. His deft hands spread them out, arrange them, and sort them; in a few seconds I have before me a rainbow of colours, all equally tempting.

Then there are those who arrive with small despatch cases, like the spivs selling bootlaces in the street. Out of them they produce tiny samples, often only the size of postage stamps, and one has to rummage to find treasure. Particularly in the spring, when the prints run riot gaily amid the plain materials which are the basis of the collection, all this leads to a delicious confusion.

As in the world of *couture* itself, it is the big firms which supply the best quality, colour, and design. The fabrics they put forward naturally influence the collection which is to come, but they themselves have been suggested by the past collection, so they ensure the continuity of fashion from season to season.

At this moment I have no idea what materials I shall be wanting in two months' time. Paradoxically enough, this makes it quite easy for me to choose. Instead of hesitating between what I think will be useful and what I think I want, I am able to decide between what pleases me and what doesn't. I give way to my instinctive reactions.

Contrary to popular belief, it is rare for a *couturier* to commission a material specially from the manufacturer. Of course materials can be inspired by stray conversations between *couturier* and manufacturer and by desires vaguely expressed several months before. For that very reason I am always very anxious to avoid proposing themes, material, or shades of colour too precisely in our casual chats. For one thing, I am well aware of the impermanence of my own whims; for another, in such an essentially collective business as *couture*, I do not want to lose the benefit of the interaction of many different ideas and views.

It is from amongst this profusion of materials which I have selected two months before that I have to make my first choice, in the interval between the displaying of the sketches and the emergence of the *toiles,* followed by a second for the more exotic fabrics. First of all I eliminate everything which definitely does not please me and which is therefore encumbering the studio to no purpose. The rest of the stuffs continue to submerge it with their mounting waves. I then mark my favourites with a cross and have them put in special cases. Of course I know perfectly well that I shall find new favourites every day whose charms I passed over at first, and which all at once I find irresistible. Nevertheless, the foundations of my selection have been laid, and all these glistening, alluring rolls, dangerous by their very beauty, are now controlled and categorized by colour and type, and also, if possible, by the manufacturer. They inundate my studio. They also illuminate it.

Surrounded by my staff, I now concentrate entirely on the problem of the mannequin still in her *toile.* Amidst all these engulfing materials, there must be one which suits both the dress and the girl. I have to resist many insidious temptations: sometimes it is the colour which attracts me, sometimes the texture of the material. Of the two, the latter is the more likely to captivate me because I never choose a material solely because of its exquisite shade of colour but more often because its texture seems exactly adapted to the effect I want to achieve. A number of factors have to be taken into consideration; the suppleness or the 'body' of the stuff, the weight or the thickness. The material is stretched out straight and on the cross; it is weighed, stroked – for it must not scratch the skin; rubbed – for the dye must not come off; and examined in the light – for the colour must suit the complexion of the mannequin who is going to wear it. What examinations, what tests it has to pass before it is deemed worthy of being chosen!

There are probably eight or nine of us altogether there in the studio. Facing me stands a lone mannequin dressed in white cotton canvas in front of a large looking-glass; behind me are two designers. Mme Raymonde is busy hunting for the material which most nearly corresponds to my scarcely formulated desire, with the help of Claude, her assistant. Mme Marguerite is supposed to remain at my side, but cannot sit still on her chair. Unable to mask her impatience, she runs up and down between the model and her post, to which I keep recalling her. By the mannequin stands the *première* or the tailor who is responsible for making the *toile*. In a corner stands Jeannine, nicknamed 'Boutonnette', who is in charge of the accessories (her hour has not yet come), and Frontine, pencil in the air, ready to make the notes destined for the files. From time to time Mme Bricard emerges out of her hatboxes, sails in magnificently, gives one definitely adverse comment, condemns an unfortunate stuff with a look, or suddenly plumps for a daring colour.

But most of the time this ritual, which would baffle an outsider, consists of choosing, from thirty black wools all of excellent quality, the sole one which is in fact suitable. As I hesitate between the rival claims of the various stuffs which are submitted to me, and try to formulate my ideas, in turn the pieces of material are draped over the shoulders of the mannequin, so that I can judge the softness and fall of the material in relation to the *toile* which is still visible on the other shoulder.

Certain combinations are obviously immediately unsuitable. 'Oh no – take that off at once.'

And I point to another piece of stuff. This one, instead of immediately sliding off the mannequin's bust, stays there. We all look at it. Does it really suit her? It certainly seems to … But after all, perhaps not. So I ask anyone at random:

'What do *you* think of it?'

They know perfectly well that I do not really want to hear their opinion, and probably don't answer me seriously. All the same, their mere presence is of assistance to me. Their reply, whatever it is, crystallizes my doubts. I press them further:

'And you, Boutonnette, what do *you* think of it?'

Boutonnette nods her head without committing herself; then it is Claude's turn, and in this way the whole room joins in, from Mme Marguerite down to the mannequin who, as the debate continues, begins to feel the first prickings of fatigue. The choice is made at the price of universal tension in which all present partake. It only needs the indifference of one person to destroy the whole climate of passionate collective research. Sometimes the decision is taken almost at once; sometimes there are dozens of false tries: in the end, we may revert to something we had previously dismissed as hopeless, after rummaging among the discarded pieces of material. Wretched fabric! Once again it is draped, re-draped, examined, and re-examined. It is never manipulated by the same hand twice; a dozen hands are there to wreak their will upon it. At last, like an umbilical cord, the length is cut. The dye has been cast, the model's fate is decided! Mme Raymonde returns to her seat, registers the material in her book, makes a note that she must tell the manufacturer, and passes the docket to Frontine who will have it filed.

Sometimes a dress is christened at the very moment of its birth, but we generally prefer to wait until we know it better before giving it a name: the baptism of a dress has a sort of sacramental quality.

We may now either pass on to the next *toile*, or take the same one all over again and choose a second material for it: a particularly striking *toile* may give birth to a whole trend of models in a variety of different colours and materials. At the same time as a second choice is made, I hastily draw, on a corner of a table, the details which will make the new model different from the previous one, unless I postpone deciding them until I have seen my reactions to the first fitting.

Now another mannequin enters. Perhaps as many as fifty or a hundred pieces of material will have to be unrolled to suit her. One visualizes the dress in grey, in pink, in green, first in matt and then in shiny black … No, none of them will do! The only thing that has been decided so far is the weight and feel of the material, for the shape of the *toile* has decided that in advance. The bales of cloth mount upon the floor; they seem to get uglier and uglier; time passes; silence falls. I no longer fire off questions, and my gestures of command become curter and curter. Finally, I decide to put off making my choice until the next day.

Once I am at home, I find myself thinking about the debatable *toile* in the middle of the night – those collection-haunted nights which turn the days into a single feverish sarabande. The next day I do actually manage to reach a decision.

In spite of all this concentration, it does sometimes happen that materials which have been chosen with the greatest possible care are found to have kept some unexpected revelation in reserve when the dress is sewn together. *Couture* is the marriage of design and material. There are many instances of perfect harmony – and there are a few of disaster.

— 7 —

THE BIRTH OF THE COLLECTION

Practically speaking, it is in the course of the ten days and also, for me, ten nights, during which the selection of the materials is going on, that 'the line', or to be more precise 'the lines', are decided. An all-round-the-clock collection is not developed on a single theme, but on seven or eight principal motifs. It must have an agreeable variety, and at the same time present a general harmony so that it never contradicts itself. This is why half the models which are made, never reach the actual collection. Our first enthusiasm encourages us to put far too many *toiles* into execution: later we have to destroy a great number of them.

Now the models are put through the intricate process of construction. At the moment when life is about to be breathed into the new creation, one has to reconcile two apparently irreconcilable forces: personality and discipline. The workrooms fall upon the *toiles* which have been allotted to them with enthusiasm. There are interminable telephone conversations with the manufacturers. This length of material has turned out to be insufficient: more must be supplied immediately; but when it does arrive, it does not conform to the original width. Fury. Protestations. Mme Raymonde strives endlessly against delays, errors, disappointments, and impatience. Marguerite revises and corrects mistakes. Meanwhile I await the results in a fever of anxiety.

My anxiety is prolonged during five or six whole days. Neither Marguerite nor I know exactly when it will come to an end. Our meetings and conversations are along the same lines as those of a nurse and a father-to-be. Every time she sees me, she knows that I will not be able to resist putting the inevitable question:

'What will they be like? And when will they be ready?'

Finally, the models are ready, and on the one day I had not expected them.

When they arrive, our hearts are in our mouths: for whereas the *toiles* have the charm of a rough sketch, leaving the imagination free to conceive the rest, what we are now being faced with is the grim reality. I must say at once that we are sometimes bowled over by what we see – and sometimes appalled! Most frequently we calculate with irritation the work which still needs doing before the dress which we are contemplating approaches anything like the figment of our imagination. Some of the dresses have been irretrievably ruined. We find them indecent, we almost want to insult them, because they seem to mock us. There are cries of:

'It's ghastly! It's an outrage! Into the wastepaper basket with it! Away with it to the dustbin!'

On the other hand, by way of compensation, there are some which look so delicious from the start, one would almost like to hug them.

'It's a dream,' we cry, as if we are gazing at the work of quite another hand than our own. 'It really is a success.'

I have often thought what an extraordinary impression this passionate vocabulary would produce on the ignorant spectator; satisfaction is expressed without shame, disappointment without limits. In order to understand these violent reactions, you have to have shared our joys, our anxieties, our hopes, our long nights of weary but painstaking toil. You would then have no doubts that ours is a labour of love.

I now seat myself once more in my chair, with a large glass in front of me. I have each new entry announced to me by the rather pompous-sounding phrase:

'Monsieur, un modèle.'

This announcement plays the same part as the three knocks which precede the raising of the theatre curtain in France. Thanks to it, I have the full benefit of the first impact of the dress; by making a grand entry like a distinguished guest, the mannequin can use all the resources at her disposal for making an effective impression. My surroundings fade away. The model is alone on centre stage.

After absorbing this first all-important impression, I ask the mannequin to come nearer, to walk towards me, so that I can examine the dress in motion. I then inspect it in the large mirror opposite me, which gives me another angle on it. The mirror shows up its faults ruthlessly. Mme Marguerite, who has already repaired a great number of them behind the scenes, notices them at the same time as me, and instinctively steps forward to correct them. I have to keep waving her back with my stick, forcing her to sit down, so that I can thoroughly saturate myself in the feel of the dress in absolute tranquillity.

The *première* is there, very often accompanied by the girl who has sewn the dress. They have brought what is left of the material with them, including the odd pieces left over from the cutting out, which I can use, if need be, to remake the sleeves, or the collar, or a pocket. But before passing to these details, I order the mannequin to continue showing the dress. I make her walk forwards, backwards, and twirl round. I examine the back, the sides, the fit of each section in turn. Finally, I ask myself:

'Is this really how I intended the dress to be?'

It is vital to make no concession to self-esteem at this point – one's own or the *première*'s, one must judge implacably. This requires a great deal of concentration. A *basque* worries me – does that mean its proportions are wrong? Should I make it shorter? No, after all, it needs lengthening. It is the skirt or the sleeves which need their length altering. Then the *décolleté* has to be deepened or lifted. Finally the proportions are judged perfect. The balance between them may only need altering by one fraction of an inch, but it makes all the difference to the success of the model. Placed at a certain point on the body, a seam may produce an enlarging effect. An infinite adjustment, and it gives an impression of slimness. All these modifications tend towards simplification. Here, a seam is apparently useless, so it is removed; there, some pleats look insignificant: they are replaced by *travail au fer* or more cunning use of the fall of the material. It is one of the great secrets of *haute couture* that a well-cut dress is the dress which contains the least cuts.

In order to facilitate the fittings, the dresses arrive at the studio, entirely covered with *fils de sens*. These threads, in contrasting colours to the material, in order to show up, have been sewn through all the pieces which make up a dress, one following the grain of the material and the other at right angles to it. The bias lies between the two. The *fils de sens*, pitiless critics, reveal all the possible faults of the cut, and make balance essential. To achieve the *faux-sens* – neither quite on the cross, nor quite on the straight, requires the hand of a master. It is to the *couturier* what dissonance is to the musician. Badly handled, a *faux-sens*, which can give the whole dress its character, forfeits that character completely.

Little by little, the fitting gets under way. Balances are rectified, proportions adjusted. Finally, bristling with pins, studded with pieces of cotton *toile*, fluttering with pieces of material cut on the cross, which indicate the position of the principal seams, or the position of alterations, the dress leaves the studio. It had entered it, apparently so glorious; it departs almost unrecognizable.

What follows has the quality of a miracle for me. The workrooms seem to be able to decipher an unbreakable code. They keep their heads among a forest of pins, apparently stuck in completely haphazardly, and a spider's web of threads. I have never been able to understand how they manage it. Nevertheless it is a fact that at the first rehearsal, the dress appears, with all the desired alterations faithfully carried out, and ready, if necessary, for new ones.

Imagine a manuscript perpetually erased, and indefatigably recommenced. At the first fitting, the dress never looks anything like how one had pictured it: either the instructions for making it have not been correctly carried out, or the material has not behaved as one had supposed it would. Effects which had been completely satisfactory in the white canvas of the *toile*, carried out in the actual fabric, reveal glaring defects. A mistake in quality, or colour, obliges me to begin all over again. After the first fitting, however, one does begin to have an idea of how the dress will look in the end. After surveying it from every angle, and considering every possible kind of alteration which might improve the dress, I finally steel myself to let it go back to the workroom. An epoch in its life has ended, but it will be followed by several more – the first rehearsal, the dress rehearsal, and the Press Show. Henceforth, I will follow the progress of each dress like an anxious father – proud, jealous, passionate, and tender – suffering agonies on their behalf. They have absolute power over me, and I live in perpetual dread that they will fail me.

During this period of the fittings, I am worried by one thing – in the course of all these alterations, these tortured doubts and fears, have I abandoned my first idea of the dress?

I am in a terrible mood all this time: my faithful staff tiptoe about the studio, terrified of letting a pin drop, trying to make themselves invisible and also trying to do everything they can to help me. At the end of several days, we come to the conclusion there are enough 'showable' dresses ready to make up a general rehearsal. It takes place in the actual *salon* where the show will ultimately be held, and has a tremendous importance in my eyes for the first time: the dresses follow after each other more or less as they will do on 'The Day'.

This rehearsal takes place in the big *salon*, which will later be crowded by the public. Against the luxury of this new setting, most of them now come into their own, but a few of them founder. There are *salon* optics, just as there are theatre optics: the dresses generally need simplification and amplification to suit them. A certain detail, which had looked charming in the studio, now becomes superfluous; a certain width, which seemed to be sufficient, now has to be exaggerated, in order to gain its true effect. After all – it is here in the *salon* that the model has to make an impression on the Press, seduce the eye of the client, and make its kill. At the same time a dress which is conceived entirely in order to shine in the *salon*, misses its basic point, which is to be worn.

The effect of the ceremonial entry of each mannequin, which I have already described in the studio, is greatly enforced at the rehearsal. I attach a great deal of importance to the shock which each model produces when it first appears in the door of the *salon*. If my satisfaction is complete, I immediately choose a hat for it: if not, I make the mannequin parade back and forward once or twice, while I examine the dress from all its angles. It often takes several minutes to discover exactly where the fault lies. In most cases, it is a case of an error in the proportions, and an excess of complication. I do not let the dress go until I have corrected it. Fashion is above all a question of line; from the shoes to the hat, the silhouette must be viewed as a whole.

That is why Mme Bricart and I now pore over the choice of the hat, whose shape has only been vaguely suggested in the sketch. The particular shape and size which will suit the 'line' of the dresses has to be decided. Before me is a huge heap of assorted shapes which are to the hats what the *toiles* are to the dresses. As in the case of the models, the details will come later. At first, all that is necessary is that the hat should suit both the mannequin and the dress for which it is to be the complement. Sometimes the problem seems insoluble. Twenty solutions are tried without success; sometimes in desperation one abandons the fruitless search among the existing shapes in order to create a hat which will suit the dress and the face, out of one's own head.

It may seem odd that we should go to all this trouble over a hat when women are in fact wearing them less and less. In my opinion, this regrettable departure is due to a reaction against those miserable pieces of headgear, in straw, bedizened with plumes and flowers, with which women disguised the poverty of their wardrobe during the war. Personally I consider that a women without a hat is not completely dressed. The fact that very young girls can get away with being hatless has encouraged their mothers to imitate them. But they are simply depriving themselves of an agreeable addition to their appearance and are apparently not sufficiently aware that the cry:

'How pretty you look today!' often means no more than:

'How well your hat suits you!'

It would be out of the question to show a collection without hats. However ravishing their dresses, the mannequins would still have a dowdy air. This is not an exaggeration: there are circumstances where one can afford to neglect the added style which a hat gives to the face, but on no account when one is presenting a new line, when proportion is all important.

The first rehearsal necessarily only includes a small number of models. They are chosen from among the most representative of the *toiles*, or those which have to be sent away to be embroidered. These last, which are always of a very simple cut, are urgent. It is not sufficiently understood that embroidery is still done by hand, as in the eighteenth century (sometimes even on the same frames) and takes a month or three weeks. A ball dress may be entirely covered with millions of *paillettes*, or pearls, each one has to be put on separately.

To return to the collection: I watch twenty dresses go by, of as varied types as possible. Then I go to sleep, with a more or less peaceful conscience, deciding to wait till morning before making a definite decision. It is astonishing how the passing of one night permits one to isolate that which one did not really like, from that which one adores! The models which I choose the next morning, will furnish the major theme of the coming collection. It is only now that I can really start to think seriously about the new line – up till now it has scarcely seemed real to me.

From first rehearsal to further fitting, the collection now follows its predestined course. An indisputably pretty dress gives birth to three or four versions, which are directly inspired by it; another, which up till now had been considered as classic, suddenly seems too studied and already out of date. So we progress, with good days, and bad days, enthusiasms, and revulsions, sometimes even disasters. In the midst of all these contradictory emotions, comes the moment when we have to suppress pitilessly all the models which we do not really like. These are the dresses which do not tie in with the others, and they have to be sacrificed to the unity of the collection even if they would have sold extremely well. It is significant that as the collection takes shape, one gets completely attuned to the lines which make it up. Nothing seems new to us any longer. As the date of the show approaches, one only knows that the dresses are well made: one has no idea whether they possess any creative interest. We have to be wary of that over-faithful companion whose presence makes everything seem out of date – habit.

The little world of the avenue Montaigne is thoroughly worn out by this time, and also burning with enthusiasm. One compliment is enough to dissipate all the effects of overworking, a reproach provokes cries of despair. The *première* who sees her dress 'thrown in the wastepaper basket' immediately bursts into tears as if she had committed a crime. With the natural and touching blindness of a mother, she looks on the model as her child and refuses to admit that this child can be at fault. Disgusted with life she is ready to hand in her notice; two hours later the same *première* will supervise a difficult task and carry through a new inspiration miraculously.

Every day the fever mounts: new crises arise which I have to calm down. I nearly kill myself repeating over and over again that if the models go wrong it is after all my fault and nobody else's, certainly not the fault of the workroom responsible for making them. This argument gets me nowhere; everyone is still convinced that I am profoundly unjust. This is the really exhausting stage, when the doctor who looks after the welfare of my workers finds the character of the ailments he has to treat has abruptly changed. No more rheumatism, no more pains in the stomach; nothing but tenacious migraines due to fatigue, and fingers wounded in the cause of wounded pride. Scarcely bothering about their appearance mannequins fling themselves into the lift, or not even bothering to wait for it, bound up the steps to their particular workroom. They would lay down their lives in order that everything should be ready on the day.

In the evening when there is peace at last in my office, and the whole building has quietened down, I reflect on all these joys and sorrows which reflect my own. I frequently feel remorse, because quite frankly I have to pronounce some harsh words during this period, in spite of all my care to be tactful. The *première* whose two models I have annulled, one after the other, without taking into account the fact that they both came from the same workroom, has had to return twice over to her girls in despair. No doubt she feels a good deal of chagrin, and a quite unjustified sense of shame. The mannequin, whom I have told that her dress does not suit her, feels herself slighted. Of course they know in their hearts that it is my aim to make them as pretty as possible, and they themselves often feel that a model does not do them justice; but sometimes they refuse to admit it!

Then, there are the deputations. Mme Raymonde comes furtively into my office in order to warn me:

'I think you ought to say a kind word to Eleanor – her dress wasn't as bad as all that …' or:

'You were really too hard on Mme Marguerite; she feels completely discouraged.'

Then it is Mme Marguerite's turn to appear; escorted by one of the *premières,* she comes to plead the cause of a dress which has been abandoned.

'Do let me keep it, Monsieur Dior. I swear to you that it will be a success. I swear I will save it.'

It is a tricky decision to have to make. On the one hand one risks succumbing to the charm of an attractive, but for some reason unsuitable dress; on the other of allowing lethargy to lead to injustice.

Problems of a different nature arise. *A couturier* who aims to present a two-hour dramatic spectacle without benefit of either plot or interval, is faced with trials undreamt of by the ordinary theatrical producer. One dress, eliminated two days before the actual show, can set in motion a cascade of changes on the blackboard in the studio where all the names of the mannequins are inscribed. The order, rhythm, and balance of the show will be affected. The programme is drawn up during the various fittings and the rehearsals and is subject to certain very important laws; each mannequin must wear the same number of dresses of each category; dark and light dresses have to alternate wherever possible – although the light dresses are generally less numerous; the models which we guess will sell in large numbers, must be judiciously arranged and alternated with the spectacular models.

Suddenly the rhythm of the collection becomes more peaceful. Everyone in the building is so hard at work, that the house is almost silent with concentration. The noise appears to be stunned. Now that we are on the eve of the dress rehearsal, we have arrived at the penultimate act of the play. The story is therefore reaching its climax.

— 8 —

THE DRESS REHEARSAL

Although the *répétition générale* or dress rehearsal absorbs me completely, it is true to say that I do not watch it. I would be incapable of describing it, and so would any of my assistants who are at my side. One of them might just be able to remember that 'Gitane' was rechristened 'Habanita'. Another might remember the name of a model which was sent back to the workroom, or needed its buttons changing; but to talk to us, you would never think that any of us had been actually present at the spectacle. In reality everybody devours it with their eyes. Those present are Mme Marguerite, Mme Bricart, the indispensable Mme Raymonde, my secretary Josette Widmer, Mme Luling, who looks after the sales, my two designers, and five assistants. To them are added M. de Mausabré and M. Donati, who are in charge of public relations, and two or three *vendeuses*. In one corner repose the last-minute accessories – bags, gloves, and jewels. On the other side, in the daylight shed by the window, sit the two artists who will sketch the models for publicity purposes. Roger Vivier, who has designed the shoes, sits next to the fireplace, with Michel Brodsky who is responsible for the sales organization. Finally M. Rouet and M. Chastel desert the commercial side of the business – very busy at this time – to come and breathe the air of the collection with us from time to time. But the reason we are all incapable of retaining an impression of the whole rehearsal, is that we are intent on examining individually the detail of each dress.

This is positively the last chance I have to alter my dresses: tomorrow they will be presented to the Press, and, if all goes well, slaves of their own success, they will no longer belong to me. But for a few hours longer, these are still *my* models. Obsessed by the importance of this final examination, I deliberately ignore everything that is going on around me. I see nothing except my dresses. For obvious reasons, no one who does not belong to the organization is admitted to the dress rehearsal: the tense atmosphere of these last terrible two days remains mercifully unknown to the public.

But I have on one occasion subjected our ritual to the scrutiny of an outsider. I once asked one of my friends – I chose someone totally ignorant of the world of *haute couture* – to come and sit in the shadow of the mantelpiece, and watch us at our work. Two months later, when the work on my collection had slackened, and I had a little free time, I asked him to describe what had been going on beneath my own eyes. Here is the tale which he unfolded to me.

When I first reached the landing on the first floor, I lost myself in white muslin. Successfully evading this first barrage of snow, I had to overcome a second, through which I was firmly but courteously rebuffed by a disembodied hand. I heard the murmur of the word *cabine* (dressing-room). To my right, a third and fourth curtain awaited me, which masked the entry to the *grand salon*, the aim of my expedition. I felt myself lost in an atmosphere of light and cleanliness. Furthermore, there was complete silence around me, but a silence full of rustling, rather like the silence in the theatre just before the curtain goes up. Then a hand lifted up the diaphanous curtain, and invited me to penetrate into the sanctuary.

I was immediately struck by a tremendous impression of whiteness. The whiteness reflected off the two rows of armchairs installed on my right, all covered in snow, on which several girls in white overalls were sitting. Quite free from the traditional gold and the crystal of chandeliers, the classical grey and white decoration of the walls, with their large mirrors, made me feel as if I was present at some council of ghosts. Then my eyes were dazzled by a fantastic Cinderella's trousseau, strewn on the carpet on my right. Accessories, whose beauty took one's breath away, luxuries and frivolities of every sort were there jumbled up in one delicious but ordered chaos, as though thrown down by the prodigal hand of a fairy godmother. I felt myself led by a benevolent hand and placed in a chair in the corner of the fireplace, clearly destined for me. I sat down and busied myself in trying to look as small as possible.

The *salon* was still almost empty, but very soon other people came and installed themselves. They all stared at me, and I felt them wondering:

'Who on earth is he?'

I felt myself growing smaller and smaller in the secretive atmosphere. Finally, somebody must have been given a tentative explanation of my presence, because there were shruggings of the shoulders and doubtful, polite, or interested 'Ohs' and 'Ahs'. These interrogations had taken place in low voices – heaven knows why they all spoke so softly! The delicate inspection which they made of me must have satisfied them; probably they guessed from my behaviour that I was really quite inoffensive. To my great relief, their attention was directed away from me elsewhere.

I profited from the respite to look about me; opposite me Cinderella's trousseau glowed beneath the light of the projectors disposed at the four corners of the platform. At the side, encroaching on the little *salon*, was a wardrobe stuffed with furs: I gave a mental shiver at the thought of winter. The panel on the left was occupied by a large table from which hung a profusion of belts, and which was loaded with an arsenal of jewellery. An old lady, myopic as a goldsmith, was indefatigably arranging the brooches and earrings, the rows of jet and diamonds. I suspected her of upsetting them on purpose as soon as she had finished her work, for she took such obvious satisfaction in doing it! Not far from her, a young man in a blue jacket with gold buttons contemplated the scene.

It was at this moment that the curtains billowed, or to be more exact, a young woman parted them, in order to enter. From the door, she announced:

'*Un modèle, Monsieur.*'

Then she revolved, advanced, and smiled. Amidst the gentle ripple of discreet laughter, I realized that this was a traditional joke to pass the time of waiting. I heard remarks like:

'She really must be taught to walk properly.'

'You see, *ma petite* …'

This last was greeted with a real gale of laughter. Obviously it was one of the favourite expressions of the absent master of ceremonies! As a *bon mot* it was a riotous success.

Around us, the spectacle was being got ready. The rows of chairs continued to fill up, with the exception of several armchairs in the middle, which obviously corresponded to that of the *Presidencia* at the Plaza de Toros in Madrid. The illusion of a bullfight was completed by the entry of a valet – who was enveloped in the inevitable curtain; he placed about ten clattering umbrellas on the table with the jewels, and then disappeared, fair, pink, and silent. Christian Dior's own place was recognizable by a peculiar installation: two pockets of brown holland ornamented the armchair to the left and the right. My neighbour informed me that these were for rubbers and crayons. In front of his chair, a stool supported two long pieces of paper and six pencils, sharpened like daggers. On the stool was a baton with a gold band.

I expected to read 'Christian Dior' on the back of the chair, as one reads 'René Clair' on the back of the chairs in a film studio. But there was nothing: only the rather unexpected inscription 'Noemie' on the stool. My neighbour, consulted once more, burst out laughing, and realized that I was decidedly outside the profession. 'Noemie', she told me, was simply the name of the worker from whom this stool had been borrowed. Disconcerted, I took refuge in silence.

It was extremely hot: outside, under the chestnut trees in the avenue Montaigne, the pavement was steaming. I heard one of the ladies say threateningly to another:

'No iced beer for you until eight o'clock this evening!'

My watch said 1.45. One wise man had lined up on the mantelpiece, within reach of his fingers, three packets of cigarettes, blocks of paper, pencils, and matches. Somebody remarked:

'We shan't be through until midnight.'

They were all settling themselves in as though for a long journey. At the same time, people continued to scuttle to and fro, performing some secret rite whose rules escaped me. Then a lady of commanding presence appeared, magnificently dressed, hatted, and bejewelled, who aroused general enthusiasm.

'Hat by Bricart!' somebody cried. 'Model by Bricart! Coiffure by Bricart! Dress by Bricart! Shoes by Bricart! Elegance by Bricart!'

Surely the show was about to begin. The person responsible for this flattering commotion disappeared as rapidly as she had come, only to reappear, an instant later, equally beautifully dressed, a little blue veil over her eyes, but this time wearing an open-necked short-sleeved white blouse. She sat down in front of me, and I discovered with astonishment on her collar an inscription as puzzling as the word 'Noemie' on the stool: the blouse was marked 'Gloire'. Obviously I still had to learn about the many intricacies of the dress trade.

Now a girl came in, pushing before her an apparatus on wheels from some other age, which was also enveloped in white *toile*. It looked like an ancient beach camera. Was it being got ready to project a film on one of the many screens in the room?

'Boutonnette', as everyone seemed to call her, lifted the cover; there was nothing beneath it but an inventory of buttons, similar to those of postage stamps. Now, amidst a rustling of materials and chairs, there was another sign that the show was about to begin.

Le patron (as Christian Dior is always called within the precincts of 30 avenue Montaigne) entered.

A murmur of relief from the assembled company accompanied him to his chair. He smiled, shook several hands, kissed several cheeks, took up his baton, and settled himself down. He too was wearing a white overall. Now everything seemed simple: there were exactly the right number of chairs and people, and each one of the spectators occupied a place which he or she felt was his by right (just as mine was tucked away in the fireplace!). At last, a tall boy in an overall lifted the white veil and announced:

'*Un modèle, Monsieur!*'

As if in response, another voice declaimed the words:

'San Francisco.'

And a mannequin appeared. She advanced, walked round the room with that elegant balanced movement so completely different from a soldier's march-past, and came to a standstill. As this was the opening number, I felt that it would probably be of comparatively minor importance, in the nature of a curtain-raiser, but at the same time expressive of the new line. I tried to see where the line was tending. Christian Dior said softly:

'It needs a different hat, something altogether more important. Now what exactly, I wonder?'

Now that my attention was directed towards it, I found that I had not even noticed before that there was a hat. Immobile in the centre of the *salon*, the mannequin gazed into space at a point which exists, according to the experts, about the roots of the spectators' hairline. At the same time, the guardian of the jewels, the two keepers of the hats, and a fourth assistant, sprang to life. The first fastened on an earring, the second and the third wreathed round her head a mass of black taffeta on a foundation of canvas, and a vaporous veil. Under the impact of these united attacks the mannequin blinked. Finally somebody placed the finished piece on top of her head. There were murmurs of approval saluting this collective effort. But it was still not good enough. From his seat, Christian Dior observed:

'It should be still more striking, add the flower.'

Mme Bricart demanded a less formal looking veil, Mme Marguerite called for black ribbon. One after the other they were tried, in different combinations. Apparently made of stone, the mannequin did at last let out a faint murmur when a piece of tulle ruffled her eyelashes.

'Don't tug me about like that!' she exclaimed.

Finally Dior himself stood up, patted the vast edifice, moved the pins, transformed the whole thing, and returned to his seat, murmuring:

'There, now that looks very pretty. Please stick in two large jet hatpins.'

Now at last, I saw the point of this so-called dress rehearsal: it was nothing but a delightful private party, for the express purpose of decorating a Christmas tree. The boxes on the floor contained the traditional crystal balls, and lights, and the stars. The mannequin was the elegant, dumb, splendidly indifferent tree. Everyone took part in the sumptuous preparations: the two hatters hovered with darting agile fingers round her head while the jeweller juggled with earrings and necklaces. 'Boutonnette' brandished her inventory of buttons of every size and every colour. The furriers offered their capes and coats with outstretched arms. Personally I thought the dress now looked perfect but apparently no dress was ever admitted to be perfect before that critical audience.

I was mistaken. The next model called 'Virevolte' exploded my theory of procedure. The girl entered, performed that little ballet which is called the showing of a dress, pushed detachment almost to the limits of insolence, and then stood still in silence. After a long reflective silence, Dior's baton indicated a point, somewhere high up on the neckline, and said very distinctly:

'Really, I find that very unattractive.'

Mme Marguerite stood up, with a man who was presumably the *premier* of the workroom responsible for the execution of the dress. Pins were brandished, one hand pulled the dress to the left, another stole beneath the material. The shoulders were re-examined, and the hem of the jacket was pinned. Without one downward glance for all this corrective labour, the mannequin's thoughts seemed to be altogether elsewhere. She only sprang to life when she was returned once more to her imperial isolation: then a smile returned to her lips. Dior approved the alterations.

'Now it's just right ... Yes, I like that!'

But it was obvious that he was still not quite satisfied. Something was still lacking. Restored to her elegant liberty, the mannequin glided forward, and pirouetted round. Suddenly Dior motioned to her to stand still.

'I know what it is,' he exclaimed. 'It needs two more buttons! Boutonnette!'

Wobbling slightly, the chariot was propelled forward. One, two, three, four, *five* black buttons, all absolutely identical to my inexperienced gaze, were tried in turn. The sixth was finally considered satisfactory. Two pins, corresponding to the two buttons, were placed on the jacket with a precision amounting to madness. Finally, after one last pirouette, 'Virevolte' left us. She had just reached the door, when a final command was flung after her:

'Add a black umbrella to it!'

The mannequins continued to file past. Every dress which entered aroused a particular problem: sometimes it was the dress itself, sometimes the hat, the muff, or the jewellery. Occasionally, accompanied by a flattering murmur and whispers of 'It's wonderful!' a perfectly executed model would sail through without any alterations. Dior would not detain the girl except to murmur:

'Oh, how pretty it looks. You couldn't hope to see anything more elegant!'

Time passed. The ashtrays filled up with cigarette butts marked with lipstick, the peppermint sweets had resumed their guilty circulation, the artists were making rapid accurate sketches. It was then that I noticed the procession of slips of paper. They came from the jewel table, where the telephone occasionally burred, and they circulated apparently of their own volition. The girl who answered the telephone in a low voice, was sending them from hand to hand, to their destination. The return message came back by the same route and the telephonist transmitted the sense of it to whoever was on the other end. If there was a delay between the appearance of two numbers, this toing and froing of messages would cross with a procession of nougat bars coming from some indefinable source, as if borne on the backs of ants. Once the bars had been distributed another problem arose – how to dispose of the cellophane which contained the nougat. Taking it off involved a sudden sharp crackle, which had to be quickly stifled, before anyone could complain about it. Annoyed murmurs greeted these greedy mouse-like nibbles. The *patron* gazed at his staff impatiently.

'Right? Everybody ready now? Roger? Claire?'

Finally, somebody opted for the heroic solution and offered a nougat to Dior himself, which at least had the effect of smoothing away his frown. Scarcely had he taken it – with a grateful smile –

than a concert of rustling paper broke out. The tension broken, the announcer cries:

'*Un modèle, Monsieur.*'

The rhythm of the show is restored. The mannequin divests herself of her jacket and lets it hang gracefully down at the end of her arms. The remarks begin to fly:

'That bow should be more important. It doesn't seem to fasten to anything.'

'Away with the fur. It clashes with the hat.'

'Look out, your skirt dips to the left and the petticoat is showing. Jeanne, you go and sit on the little stool, then you will see what I mean.'

'The hat is not quite sensational enough. Add a mass of black veiling.'

'Frederic, that collar is not stiff enough.'

Dior tells an assistant who is curving in the crown of a hat:

'No, leave it as it is.'

And he asks Mme Bricart, who is sitting beside him:

'What's that little thing that you've got in your hand? Yes, that. Give it to me.'

'You can't do that,' she exclaims.

'Oh yes I can.

The object now adorns the hat. Perhaps the gloves are tried and retried over and over again, or the umbrellas, which are put up, put down, put up again. Finally they are abandoned in favour of a muff. The voice of Mme Bricart extols maxims as formal as the banderillas of a bullfight.

'That one is too formal. Double the veiling. Not that one, another. No, the black one.'

One of the dresses undergoes a series of drastic criticisms from the moment it comes into the room. There is obviously too much to do, so it is sent back:

'I will look at it tomorrow,' says Dior. 'It is the last time I shall see these dresses, so I ought to look at them properly.'

Another time, the choice of a hat seems to drag on for ever. In order to justify his intransigence, Dior explains politely:

'It is not so much a question of the hat itself, but the proportions of the whole outfit.'

On another occasion, a mannequin was rudely stung to life beneath our eyes. The girl was showing a costume in shades of russet and orange with majestic slowness. Whereupon the conductor of the orchestra waved his baton to indicate:

'Walk faster!'

The mannequin's lips visibly trembled, and it was as though the marble isolation of a statue had been shattered. She overcame it bravely with the traditional smile, but before she left the *salon*, Dior was careful to reassure her:

'Don't worry. You were fine.'

As the hours wore on, attitudes grew more soporific. A gentle fatigue descended over the faces of the mannequins, who were all warmly dressed, being a season in advance of the thermometer. On all sides, remarks were being scribbled on the large sheets of paper.

'Have you noted down the diamonds in the ears? Five rows of jet ... The beaver muff ... The one Alla was wearing ...'

Occasionally, rarely, Christian Dior himself would cry out:

'This name is really impossible. *Mesdames*, suggest a name for me.'

It was a question of baptizing, or debaptizing a dress. About one of the more fantastic names, Dior said with a smile:

'If anybody asks you why it is called that, say you don't know, because, really, I haven't the faintest idea.'

As the show went on, I heard the words '*les femmes*' constantly used to make some point. Every profession has one word for designating its clients. In the world of fashion, they are simply *les femmes*, the women.

'The women won't like that,' says someone. 'The women will wear that on one side ... That is very slimming, the women will look good like that.'

This term 'the women' has a sort of universality about it; it is pronounced with a mixture of respect and love.

About six o'clock, I took advantage of the exceptional activity which was aroused by a wedding dress – there is always one in every collection – silently pushed aside two deserted chairs, crossed the *salon* and slipped out behind the white curtains. In the avenue Montaigne, the sun was shining. Having just left such a wintry scene, I found the women who passed in their summer dresses paradoxically summery. I felt a sudden mad desire to buttonhole them and say:

'No, that revers will not do at all! It's far too long.'

At the same time, I felt a certain pride. I was the depository of a secret, which in a few weeks' time would transform the most elegant of the women who were passing. I cast one more backward glance towards the windows of the house, behind which I knew that the showing would go on for several hours, until night fell and the first stars came out. Until, in fact, that moment of inspiration and exhaustion which authors and actors both experience on the eve of the battle, when they feel at the same time drained of everything and miraculously enriched.

— 9 —

THE EVE OF THE BATTLE

The moment comes for the new line to be baptized. The baptism takes place in the three days which separate the dress rehearsal from the opening show. I draw up the Press release, describing the season's trend, trying to express it in as precise and unliterary language as possible. In order to think of the title, and the emblem which will crown the new fashions, I give myself over to last-minute inspiration. In fact I arrive at the name which concretizes the tendency of the day by thinking in terms of the most marked silhouette of the collection, sacrificing the truth and my hatred of extremes to the modern taste for a slogan.

In spring 1955 for example I picked on the fullness in the skirts of certain models, to isolate the letter A, which succeeded the letter H of the preceding season. The letter Y indicated the lengthening of the skirt, the slimming of the figure, and the high position of the bust, between the two branches of the Y. But each collection consists of a great variety of themes, and one letter – A, H, or Y – cannot represent them all. So whatever the name with which the collection is christened, I write about four pages to indicate the main trends of the season. I try to write as soberly as possible, but how can one avoid altogether the traps into which the language of fashion are apt to lead one? I am afraid I always end up by falling into them. After enumerating the principal characteristics of the new fashion, I detail those of the accessories, including trimmings, hats, furs, belts, jewellery, buttons, gloves, umbrellas, shoes, stockings, and hairstyles.

Meanwhile the workrooms are in a positive fever of last-minute activity. They are now on the eve of the ordeal for which they have been preparing for four trying months. It is the moment when the models which one had definitely decided to suppress, have a way of reappearing. From time to time they come before me, interrupting my work as a fashion journalist, in order to try and creep back into favour. Sometimes it is the mannequin, and sometimes the *première*, who sponsors their return to grace. Often I agree, and congratulate them on their persistence; models whose future I tried to blight like an unnatural father, now go forward and have a glorious career. Severity for its own sake is quite as dangerous as excess of indulgence.

Wherever I go at this time, I see only dresses. They have passed before my eyes too many times, occupied my thoughts too much, for it to be possible for me to judge them impartially any longer. The whole collection seems a failure to me and although seventy models have been registered, I have the sensation of having done nothing, or, to be more exact, accomplished nothing.

It is in fact in order to prove to myself the contrary, that I reserve for myself the task of drawing up the charts which are hung over the dressing-table of each mannequin on the day of the show. These charts contain the number and name of each dress, followed by a brief description and the detailed indication of the accessories, all indispensable references to the dresser.

The order of the show is also indicated on the charts; this obeys certain fixed laws of precedence. First come the suits, then the formal town dresses, then the more formal outfits, the cocktail dresses, the short evening dresses, finally the long evening dresses and the ball gowns, which are generally spectacularly embroidered. The wedding dress ends the show. But to give it a certain dramatic quality, one sometimes includes certain town dresses or particularly expressive suits among the cocktail dresses. As for the shocking models, those which are designed to draw attention to the new line, they are shown towards the middle of the show. It is the custom to call them the 'Trafalgars', those which make the covers or big pages of the magazines. It is these models which determine the fashion of today, and also that of tomorrow. After an hour of the show, they recapture the wandering attention of the audience.

These 'Trafalgars' have a curious fate. Perhaps some of them will never be worn in real life. Others will have their success 'late in life' and will only come into their own in the next collection. Others will be so quickly adopted, worn, and lived in, that six months later people will wonder what was considered so extraordinary about them.

In drawing up the programme of the collection, I pull my ideas about it into shape not so much for the benefit of the public, whose reactions remain marvellously unpredictable, but for my own benefit. I cannot feel myself satisfied if I have made no concessions. At this late stage, I still eliminate several more models and suppress several outfits, whose sales appeal was certain, but whose intrinsic interest was not so sure. On these dresses, I write 'Not for the Press', and take them out of the first showing, which is always too long.

All this does not take place without tears and protestations. Alla, with her inimitable hieratic bearing, stalks into my office, like Tragedy itself. She does not even have to speak; one glance from those eyes, half Slav, half Manchurian, tells me the worst:

'You want your dress put back.'

'Oh, please, Monsieur Dior. It's one of the best …'

'Don't you think, Alla, that it's rather like a suit which you wore in the last collection?'

'Monsieur, I'm sure it will be a success.'

After all, isn't this my first reaction from the public? Alla is a woman, she loves clothes and – what is not to be despised – she really understands them. I am now three-quarters of the way to being convinced. The return of Alla, wearing the dress in question, makes up my mind for me. Nevertheless, despite the wiles of mannequins and *premières* in defending their own clothes (I know all their different ruses) the interest of the collection must come first; its unity has to be preserved jealously, if its significance is not to be lost.

By now the building has become a real ant-heap. Indeed, the apprentices I find scuttling about the corridors, carrying boxes or furs, do remind me very much of ants. Busy, and meticulous, they pass each other without exchanging a single word. If one of them drops a piece of material, another stoops down to pick it up. Boys in white overalls scurry by, with tape measures round their necks. The workmen come to mend some of the gold chairs, and then the painter who is to touch up the silver letters over the entrance. This incessant circulating activity is amazing, oddest of all is the fact that it all seems to be going one way. They are all so accustomed to the labyrinthine passages of the house, that they take one staircase to go up, and another one to come down. Astonished visitors, always going in the same direction, wonder what secret machinery exists which enables the same people to pass before their eyes four times within a quarter of an hour.

My staff has adopted the vigilant seriousness which belongs to the acolytes of an important ceremony. The mannequins, who throughout the year were to be found hanging about in laughing groups, now proceed down the corridors leading to the big *salon*, with frowning brows and a noticeable air of absorption. For my own part I no longer have the time to say to them:

'How are you, my dear?' or:

'Not too tired, I hope, *ma petite*.'

The *Service de la Presse* in its turn burdens me with its worries. The showing of a collection has this in common with the opening of a play: the first contact with the opinion of the specialists has an exceptional importance. I believe it is true to say that the chroniclers of fashion generally show more skill than the theatre critics. That does not stop the *couturier* from brooding over his collection with the feelings of an author whose piece is just about to face the firing squad. Twice a year I have to endure this terrible torment. Some people find it adds piquancy to the game. Personally, I hate it, just as I used to hate examinations. My friends, in order to comfort me, keep up the pretence that this appalling hurdle constitutes the best defence against growing old. I pretend to believe them …

As the great day draws near, the nerve centre of the building shifts from the studio to the *salon*. The publicity department becomes the heart which beats out unrest into the general bloodstream; M. de Mausabré and M. Donati descend one floor to cope with the special circumstances of the opening. They are battling with Homeric problems of precedence: into two rooms and a landing, they have to squash three hundred people, when, allowing a narrow corridor for the mannequins, there is at most room for two hundred and fifty. A just and complicated hierarchy governs the rules by which one guest is sacrificed to another: and it is in fact our dearest and most intimate friends who find themselves relegated to the doorways, corners, and staircases. Even if it is blocked by a hat or a shoulder, the eye of friendship is the eye of indulgence. At least – so we hope!

The exact placing of each seat is a study in itself. There are the *habitués*, whom any change will mortally offend, the writers who have switched over from one paper to another, friends who have fallen out with each other from one season to the next, the papers which have either sprung into existence since the last collection, or else grown in importance. To each journalist must be allotted the place which is suitable both to the importance of the paper for which they write, and to their personal prestige. Even so, the plan of the seating in the *salon* sometimes has to be modified owing to unforeseen circumstances. For example, an American agency once added this charming postscript to its usual demand for a place:

'Mrs X would like to have a comfortable armchair in the little *salon*, near the exit, because she is expecting a baby at about the same time as your collection is due to be shown, and she would like to be able to leave the *salon* easily without disturbing anyone else in case of an emergency.'

Although some of the guests ask for places on the staircase, because they are subject to claustrophobia, on the whole it is the first row of seats in the *grand salon* which are the most sought after. In order to please everybody, *Service de la Presse* has to understand how to say 'no' politely in every language.

In my office the pink slips of paper which help me to fix the prices of the clothes, are beginning to pile up. It will perhaps come as a surprise to learn that I concern myself personally with the prices, when as a rule I have nothing to do with the administration or the sales side of the business. But the price of a dress is of fundamental importance. Every model is the subject of a detailed dossier, stating the hours of work spent on it, the cost of the work done by hand, and the price of the material. By adding to this a percentage of the overheads, taxes, and the necessary amount of profit, one gets a very good idea of the price at which the dresses ought to be sold.

But these prices, although fairly calculated, are not necessarily the right prices. A dress which is apparently insignificant, may have taken far longer to make than another which is far more striking. As a dress ought to be sold as far as possible at a price which corresponds to its appearance, I have to lower the commercial price of the one, and increase that of the other. Very often it is those little wool dresses, those casual dresses, which necessitate the greatest sacrifices. One can hardly demand a great price for them, yet the making of them – particularly when they are pleated – is one of the most laborious tasks we have to face. Yet how can we admit to our clients that 'a casual little day dress' needs as much care and attention as a ball dress, sensationally draped and tucked?

With prices fixed, publicity under control, the collection christened, the final fittings accomplished – the last evening before the opening which is generally prolonged far into the night, and which we call the 'eve of the battle', arrives at last. Nerves are on edge, and we are all at the end of our tether. On the one hand, one panics: nothing will be ready, everything will go wrong, we are on the verge of catastrophe. On the other hand, one is convinced, optimistically, irrationally, and even fatalistically, that everything will really be all right. Anyway it is too late to do anything about it now!

I ask several friends to rally round and support me during the evening. They come to my studio and sit around on stools and chairs. The lamps round the mirrors shine brightly. The last embroidered dresses arrive in pieces and are hastily put together as they appear. The mannequins, dazed with fatigue, don them quickly, and begin to turn slowly round in front of the mirrors, like mayflies, in the halo of light which stings our tired eyes. I look at Renée, wilting a little. Her smile is becoming more and more strained but one last detail has to be altered before the fitting is finished. Like me, she will stick it out. When she vanishes, when the last pin has been inserted, Claire takes her place. She has tried the wedding dress, which completes the collection, on once more: it is always she who wears it, and I do not despair of seeing her in it when she is a grandmother, for she is a young bride personified.

Now the last-minute dresses begin to arrive: these are the models which have been planned after the dress rehearsal, either to accentuate a predominant trend, or to fill in a gap in the programme. These are real miracle dresses. I have known them to be designed one evening and ready the next morning, against all seeming possibility.

It is also the turn of the last-chance dresses. Victoire comes in, as if about to join battle. The very way in which she wears the contested model shows that she has sworn to return triumphant. With a confident, slightly cheeky smile, she traces a pirouette and pretends to hesitate modestly half-way.

As the hours pass, fatal weariness creeps over me. Harassed, practically dried up of all ideas, I have to keep my attention rigid until the last dress has been passed. Piles of sandwiches and cakes circulate, and glasses of red wine. Curiously enough a sense of well-being now begins to creep over one, born of exhaustion, doubts too long entertained, and the happiness of feeling oneself among one's fellow workers. Only essential comments are pronounced. Despite one's fatigue, one savours the sensation of having brought a joint labour to a triumphant conclusion. Yet still it is not finished: there are still a few more models to be inspected – there always seems to be one more, and we all have to sit down again.

About three o'clock in the morning we bid each other affectionate farewells. Burning with tiredness, with our spirits disturbed, but our consciences at rest, we can at least feel that we have done our best.

— 10 —

THE SHOWING OF THE COLLECTION

I usually find it very difficult to wake up, but it is no hardship on this particular morning, in spite of the late hour I went to bed the night before. I want to arrive as early as possible at the avenue Montaigne. It is generally beautiful golden August weather when we show the winter collection and, outside number 30, Paris is in the full bloom of summer. I stop outside the house a moment in order to gaze at the facade, reflecting on the spectacle which will so soon be put on inside it. I am impatient to see the *grand salon*, which is still empty, empty of all those who will shortly fill the rows and rows of gilded chairs. Jostling one behind the other, one close beside the other, they seem to stamp their golden feet, and wait. The flowers attract my attention: I am too fond of them not to take this opportunity of indulging my particular whims: I ask for a rose here, a carnation there. Further on, I have a stained armchair removed, and I pick up a forgotten thread off the carpet. Robert de Mausabré advances across the *salon*, in order to pour into my ears the history of the latest drama which has obliged him to alter his seating arrangements once more. I calm him, and go down to the *boutique*.

There, also, work has gone on all through the night. When I left the house in the early hours of the morning, I had already seen a rough outline of what was going to be done, and I gave several pieces of advice and encouragement. I find all the workers there now, dead beat, but above all anxious to know if I approve of what they have done. As in the case of the flowers, I ask for several little changes of detail:

'Not enough positive colour!'

'Pull out some more scarves!'

Trying to look at everything at once, I rush hither and thither, distributing remarks over my shoulder:

'Move the dummy which is blocking that window full of gloves!'

'Why have you put a dark dress near the door? You want a light one there instead.'

All the time I am trying to revive their spirits. The opening of a collection is a festival; the decor which surrounds it should suggest gaiety and fantasy – down to the aroma of the rooms:

'Spray some more scent!'

By now it is nine o'clock. Through the window I can see the street and the chestnut trees, dappled by the sun. Cars are beginning to fill the pavements, and groups of people are forming outside the doors, as friends recognize and hail each other. Laughter and greetings fill the air, before they finally decide to go inside. All our visitors have been obliging enough to get up very early this morning, and as they come to watch the show, they have a holiday air. I am grateful to them – but heavens, how terrified of them I feel!

In the studio three or four models are waiting for me, to which the girls have been putting the finishing touches since six o'clock this morning. These are generally coats, intended to complete a *toilette*, or the famous embroidered ball dresses, which always arrive late. Inspecting them helps me to kill time, until the grim moment when I have to face my inquisitors. Finished at last! I can change nothing more.

When the first guest enters the hall, he sets in motion, all unknown to him, a meticulous timetable which only ends when the complete collection has been shown. In the dressing-room, warned by messengers, and the bustle and noise of chairs scraping, of this fateful arrival, the mannequins start to flap.

'Are they arriving already?'

Between the world of the *salon* and that of the back quarters, there exists only one ultimate point of contact: that of the emotion which spreads briskly from one to the other. But before this complicity can arise, the two camps are content to observe each other suspiciously. Personally, I remain alone and ask myself over and over again:

'Have I imported enough novelty?'

'Is this novelty really "wearable"?'

'Are the models sufficiently striking?'

In fact, I am no longer capable of judging. The most exacting and capricious jury in the world is assembling on the next floor, to conduct my trial. Ought I to plead guilty? The game has now passed out of my hands, into those of my mannequins, who must henceforth act as my lawyers. It is the duty of my dresses to make them as beautiful as possible, that is to say, as eloquent as possible. It is they, in fact, who will bear witness to my character. My friends, realizing that I am undergoing the sufferings of a prisoner, come to comfort me in the dock. As they are themselves in a state of tension comparable to mine, the smiles we exchange are very far from natural.

It is a quarter to ten. In the hall, someone is spraying scent in the path of the guests, and on the first floor the *Service de la Presse*, posted at the bottom of the stairs, is distributing the programmes of the show.

In the mannequins' dressing-room, complete confusion seems to be reigning. How on earth could it be otherwise? In a space habitually reserved for twelve mannequins, and the *chef de cabine*, Mme de Turckheim, are now crammed Mme Marguerite, ten dressers, all the *premières* and tailors, three hairdressers, my two immediate assistants, and naturally the girls themselves. Around them are milling the workers who have brought down the dresses, and the young men brandishing accessories. Try to stuff them all in, immobilizing them for a minute, and you would not succeed. But bustling to and fro, carrying models, jewels, or combs, kissing each other on the cheek, pulling each other about, they somehow all manage to get in somewhere: I see it happen every morning of the opening of the collection with fresh amazement.

When I arrive, the girls, in their white overalls, are still in the midst of doing their hair, or making up. It is easy to imagine that behind the scenes of a *couture* house there is an eternal strip-tease. In fact the austerity there is even greater than behind the curtains of a theatre, and untidiness is forbidden. The girls only take off their overalls at the moment when they don their dresses, and the fugitive glimpse of their figures in girdle and brassiere is no different from that which they would offer on a strait-laced beach. On their faces, all the traces of fatigue have disappeared as if by magic. They have never looked more beautiful: they have the radiance of brides, because for six weeks they have been working up to this day. It is their duty to conquer and convince the audience, show them the new fashion, and impose it upon them.

Victoire gets ready with the studiousness of Iphigenia preparing herself for the sacrifice. Lucky concentrates intensely: for her, every entrance into the *salon* implies a metamorphosis. Sitting down, she can look overcome by overwork; standing, she looks dazzling and splendid. Lucky is fashion itself brought to life: she can make a comedy or a tragedy out of a dress as she chooses. In her corner Lia industriously paints her face, splashed with patches of red, pouting like a little girl. Somebody comes in with the news that the first important guests have arrived. Immediately, all the mirrors reflect attentive figures, concentrating entirely on the task of beautifying themselves.

Laden with flowers, illuminated by chandeliers and floodlights, the *salons* begin to fill up. The whole scene has an aspect, at once lighthearted and worldly, quite different from that found in the theatre. Here, there is no red impressive curtain, no armchairs drawn up in a neat line, whose permanent function is to convey the idea of a heavy performance. The Louis Seize chairs, in spite of their numbered cards, are obviously drawn up to watch some drawing-room comedy.

In the dressing-room, the telephone rings without stopping. Mme Marguerite is demanding the missing models from the workrooms. This has happened every season since I opened my house. Every season I try and ensure that all the models have been brought down the evening before the show, and hung up in the wardrobe. In vain – I am sure I shall never succeed! The *premières* only consent to release their cherished children at the very last moment. The night before they left them in the workrooms on the basket-work dummies in silence and obscurity.

There, they still belonged to their makers; below, their makers have the irrational feeling that they will be stolen from them. Their emotions strike a sympathetic chord in my own heart: like them I always feel a certain regret and irritation at thinking of the destiny of these dresses, into which so much loving care has been poured, which are to be shrivelled up beneath the fire of the floodlights. From this evening onwards, they will be thrown hither and thither, scorned, even trampled under foot. I am powerless to prevent it happening, but all the same it upsets me. With the exception of certain rare shows, I have never wished to see my collection again after the first day of its presentation to the public. I am frightened of meeting my old friends the models again – contact with life, the public, and commerce, will have transformed them. They will have grown too far away from me.

The *salon* is full and the staircase is filling up. Spectators are crowded on to the very last step where it is possible to see the top of Victoire's hat (she is the shortest of the mannequins) by craning their necks. From above, by leaning over the wrought iron balustrade, you can make out a complete figure if you occupy one of the first steps, the hem of a ball dress from the upper steps, and if the worst comes to the worst, only the tip of a shoe. The stairs have to be moderately empty to be comfortable. Half an hour before the show, two people are seated comfortably side by side on each step; but twenty minutes later, they have disappeared beneath a sea of new arrivals. The staircase begins to look like an overloaded boat, near to sinking. The privileged members of my staff also have their places there, some of them are on chairs on the small landing, others in the embrasures of the windows, the remainder scattered about anywhere they can find an inch of space. At the very top of the staircase can be spied a white cloud of apprentices in their overalls; they have temporarily escaped the watchful vigilance of the head of their workroom.

10.25.

I send down to Mme Raymonde to ask what state the *salon* is in. I want to know if the most important guests – those without whom the show cannot go on – have arrived yet. Yes, she sends back a message to say they are there. In a twinkling of an eye, the model girls are ready. In a fever, they range themselves in battle order in the narrow corridor which leads to the first *salon*. Feeling is intense in the dressing-room, and I think it communicates itself to the audience. Neither side knows how things are going to turn out. A gentle hiss is the discreet signal by which Mme Raymonde indicates to the first mannequin that she can start the procession. From the shelter of my curtain, I commend them to Providence!

That is the moment – after the mannequin has put on the dress, and before she shows in the bright circle of lights in the *salon* – that for the first and last time I am able to discover the significance of my clothes. However tired I am, this fleeting moment practically always brings me happiness. The girl and the dress have never seemed dearer to me. The ultimate fate of the model is still wrapped in mystery, but I am amply repaid for all my worry and exhaustion by seeing my dream come to life beneath my eyes.

There sits the public, watchful, curious, equally likely to be carried away by enthusiasm as by disappointment. People are standing up and waving at friends at the other end of the *salon*, and late-comers are looking for programmes. Sweets are being handed round. A girl makes her way among the close-packed chairs and distributes fans; cigarettes light up.

When the first mannequin enters, by some miracle everyone is sitting down, and there is actually silence. From the door, the announcer gives the name of the model, and repeats the number in English. '*Numéro quatorze*. "Écosse." Fourteen.'

The mannequin walks across the *salon*, turns, threads her way through the narrow space between the chairs, and leaves for the *petit salon*. There at the entrance, a second announcer repeats the name and number. The announcement echoes a third time on the landing.

'*Numéro quatorze*. "Écosse." Fourteen.'

Behind the grey curtain, we are in anguish, and the first twenty minutes generally pass in a silence heavy with mingled hope and anxiety. I scarcely dare ask the girls what effect they have produced.

But eventually I gain courage from the air of satisfaction and dare to pose them several leading questions. They answer positively:

'Oh yes, Monsieur Dior, that one was a *great* success.'

or:

'It certainly created a stir.'

But I do not really breathe again until the first mannequin has been clapped. That produces a legitimate smile of satisfaction: I kiss the girl concerned on both cheeks, and I think the whole dressing-room full of mannequins feels like doing the same – even though they are supposed to be her rivals. However one swallow does not make a summer, and it needs several salvoes of applause to constitute genuine enthusiasm. Then the tempo quickens. As they change, the mannequins toss me off bulletins of progress:

'It's really going well!'

'I got my claps that time!'

Trembling I try to tie them to more precise descriptions.

'Would you say it was going as well as the last collection?'

With their heads muffled in their skirts, furiously tugged over their heads in their anxiety to be ready with the next number, the girls hastily reassure me. To tell the truth they have had absolutely no chance to gauge the reactions of the public in the course of showing their numbers. Which is why their reports, though enthusiastic, are rather vague:

'I think they're getting warm.'

I remember getting an extraordinary bulletin from France, one of my previous mannequins who has since left to get married. She sat herself down, crossed her long legs in front of her, and said quite slowly and solemnly with the disconcerting directness of a child:

'That was a wow! I really vamped them!'

Of course not all the dresses are a success: the mannequins' reactions to failure vary. Tania, who is subject to mercurial changes in humour, refuses to admit defeat. When she returns from the *salon,* she swears to herself in Russian at clients so incapable of appreciating a good dress when they see one. I feel she would like to scratch their eyes out! But in most cases the mannequin silently and speedily changes her dress, impatient to get back to the *salon* and have her revenge.

Sometimes a last-minute disaster gives us all a fright. With a shaking hand, one sticks in a multitude of pins, hoping to hide from the eye of the public the unforgivable scandal of a dipping hemline. We watch the model go without daring to hope for too much. My closest assistant hands an umbrella to the mannequin; I hastily twine a scarf round her neck, intended to draw the attention of the examiners away from the hem – and the model is ready to go before the jury. Mme Raymonde's heart misses a beat when she sees the skirt dipping dangerously below the coat, but fortunately she seems to be the only one to notice.

Lucky walks forward, turns, slips off her jacket to her finger tips and lets it hang for a moment; suddenly, there is a round of applause. Sometimes it is the magic of a particular colour, or neckline which has aroused it – in any case, it has made the public blind to a sin which was after all only venial. There is such glamour about the atmosphere of a show that the spectators have been known to applaud a dress of which only one half had been embroidered, and which all unknown to them had had to be hastily redesigned to cover up the catastrophe. A simple black dress cannot summon up the same powers of suggestion since it triumphs by its very austerity.

Provided everything goes well, it is about at the thirtieth model that one begins to get the feel of the *salon*. Mme Raymonde leaves her observation post for an instant and comes and gives me the news in the dressing-room.

'Oh *patron*, *patron*, I think everything is going to be all right!'

Knowing how careful she is to reassure me the first instant it is possible to do so without being over-optimistic, I begin to take courage, only to lose it again twenty times before the end of the show.

Mme Raymonde knows the *salon* by heart: she can tell the different kinds of applause – that of the journalists from that of the friends of the house. The first comes from people who are at work there and then in the *salon*. Before letting themselves go with enthusiasm over a model they must register their appreciation in their notebook. The second type of applause is more spontaneous, if it carries less weight. Nevertheless, both types give us pleasure.

With her eyes closed, Mme Raymonde could describe the exact reception of each dress which was received with enthusiasm: she could say, for example, about the grosgrain *tailleur* with the full skirt, that the big *salon* applauded it, the little *salon* took up the applause, and the staircase was delirious. She could write a thesis 'Applause in relation to *Haute Couture*', which would consider the subject from the modest claps accorded a morning costume, to the tumultuous cheers at the end of the show, not forgetting the thunderous claps given to the elaborate ball dress.

She is also an expert in interpreting the buzz of conversation from a distance. She knows that it is made up of exclamations, both admiring and denigratory, and that chatter, when it accompanies the appearance of a mannequin, is a bad sign as it betokens a slackening of interest. On the other hand, if it comes after the applause of the experts, it prolongs and confirms their enthusiasm. Mme Raymonde's experienced hand is also seen in the cheers which she literally plucks from the audience at the end of the show in my honour. Some of my friends think them rather vulgar, inferior in quality to attentive silence; but for my own part, I must confess that I appreciate them tremendously.

Towards the middle of the show, a wave of lassitude runs through the *salons*. For half an hour, the destiny of the collection has been taking shape. The Press knows the new line by now, and is getting used to seeing it in action. Spiritually and mentally the audience feel the need to stretch. They find relief in powdering their noses. For some reason, every woman in the room seems to be seized with the idea at the same time. For sixty minutes they have been quite happy being spectators: suddenly they remember that they are there to be looked at as well. In haste they correct what they consider to be faults and pat their noses stealthily like criminals. One lights a cigarette, another makes sure that her bag is still beside her. Knees and legs uncurl, skirts are pulled into shape. A guest resumes the scarf which she had discreetly taken off.

All these details are reported to me in mime, for I never enter the *salon*. Mme Raymonde passes me a note, on which is pencilled the solitary word:

'Faster.'

And I realize that we must press on.

It is a quarter to twelve. In the dressing-room, the agitation is at its height. For several minutes, Mme Raymonde concentrates especially on the order of the show; she worries over one mannequin who is lagging behind, or another who has jumped her place in the queue, that is to say got in front of her comrades. The fateful moment when we must switch from day dresses to evening dresses has arrived.

The *coiffeurs* dance a positive ballet around the mannequins who, like all women in the grip of their hairdresser, see and hear nothing. They are all demanding false switches of hair, and I have to wait until they are delivered to collect them. Thirstily Renée demands a glass of water, and swallows it on the landing, where she runs no risk of spilling it on her dress. We argue with the dressers and interrupt each other and I chase out several apprentices who have no business to be in the dressing-room.

'*Mesdames*, will you please take yourselves off?'

The first ball gowns literally descend: they are dropped down from the gallery which runs round the dressing-room, and float gently on to the heads of those below, sometimes imprisoning someone completely. There are cries of protest and shrieks of laughter. As the mannequins line up to enter the *salon*, somebody whispers treacherously from above:

'What a pity! My dress is being worn by Magda! Jeanne would have looked so much better in it.'

I rise up in fury.

'Will you come down from there, you miserable little gremlin?'

Short evening dresses, full-length furs, full-skirted dresses, finally the grand ball dresses, encrusted with embroidery – I myself decide the order in which they are to be shown, rather as a firework artist launches the various pieces in his *répertoire*. My mannequins sail forth like a brilliant armada, all sails flying, going forth to conquer the world in the cause of the new fashion.

It is time for Claire to put on the wedding dress which completes the show. She is a born mannequin and adores her job. She has been married for several years, but of all my girls she is the one who is best fitted to play the part of the young bride. It is a difficult role, and has a superstition attached to it. The girls who work at the dress sew a lock of their own hair into the hem in order to find a husband during the coming year. The mannequins on the contrary pretend that it is unlucky to wear the dress, say that the girl who shows it will never be a bride in real life.

The mannequins are returning from the *salons* for the last time. Their gloves are stripped off, their jewels returned to their cases, and they collapse, exhausted, in front of their dressing-tables. Claire descends the minute winding staircase from the special cubby-hole, where she has gone to get ready. Helped by two apprentices who are literally engulfed in her train, she miraculously manages to cleave a way for herself through the crowded passage.

She enters the *grand salon*. The apprentices hand over the train to the maid of honour. The veil, which only a moment ago was a mere piece of chiffon, is now an ethereal cloud of white about her head. The announcer shouts:

'Grand Mariage.'

It is a signal. Silence has fallen in the dressing-room as Claire sets off on her snow-white voyage. From the humblest little seamstress to Mme Raymonde and I, we are all waiting in anguish to see how she will be received. The applause which she gets will apply far beyond her dress, to the whole collection.

Has she really shown the wedding dress already? I can hardly believe it. She has scarcely left us before the whole world seems to be on its feet. Chairs are scraped back, and there is the sound of tumultuous applause. In the chaos of abandoned chairs and spilt ash-trays, the audience splits up into little groups of people, some of whom nod their heads in agreement, while others dispute some particular point arising from the collection. The little world of *haute couture* is re-united.

Everyone makes for the *grand salon* where compliments, arguments, criticisms, and gossip are all being freely exchanged. Meanwhile the waiters are mounting the staircase bearing the champagne with which we all now drink a toast to the new fashion.

For me, the terrible moment has arrived when I have to be confronted with the voices, the laughter, the cheers, the sighs, of which up till now I have only heard the echoes behind my grey satin curtains. I abandon my vantage point and, relinquishing my momentary deafness, surrender myself up to the warmth and affection of my friends. I call it a terrible moment, because it is now that I reach the climax of the terror which I have been experiencing ever since the beginning of the show. But it is also a delicious moment, because I finally see for the first time the beloved faces of my friends, whose presence up till now I have only suspected. While the champagne circulates, I shake outstretched hands, I kiss scented cheeks, I receive the congratulations of my staff, and I listen to the delightfully exaggerated words of praise which are being applied to my collection.

'Divine!' 'Adorable!' 'Ravishing!'

My christian name is on every lip: I want to thank every single person in the room and tell them how pleased I am that I have succeeded in pleasing them. Dizzy with the noise and with my own sense of happiness, I scarcely have time to reply to the journalist who asks me which is my favourite dress.

'They are all my favourites,' I answer. 'They are my children, and I love them equally as one loves one's children ...'

The fact that I see these people twice a year, and always under such moving circumstances, creates bonds of affection between us which are closer than those of blood. I have no idea if other dress houses have the same orgy of kissing after the show is over: but being by nature a person who adores demonstrations of affection and tenderness, I know that today I kiss positively everybody on the cheek. My own cheeks are covered with lipstick, a sure sign of the success of my collection, apart from the fact that red is my lucky colour.

Changed and relaxed, the mannequins now make their way into the *salon*. I see them in their corner, sipping their champagne, still trembling slightly from the tension of the show, smiling from a mixture of nerves and satisfaction. In a moment I shall go into the dressing-room with them and toast our success jointly together with the *premières*. As my own nerves relax, I feel exhaustion creeping over me. It is almost delicious to feel so tired. I reply to the hail of questions which are being flung at me through a haze. One thought obsesses me: Oh, to be seated, and taste at last the joy of having completed the collection.

I want to shout out:

'It's done, it's finished, it's over at last!'

At the same time I realize that tomorrow I shall feel an intolerable void. My life in fact revolves round the preparation of a collection with its torments and happiness. None of this will be mine. In the respite which will be mine from tomorrow, I shall be able to experience none of this. I know that in spite of all the delights of a holiday, it will seem an intolerable gap. As the *salons* gradually empty, my thoughts stray to the dresses which so recently filled them. Who knows what tomorrow holds in store for them? They are back hanging in their cupboards, as forgotten as the empty champagne glasses. It is now that I should like to sit down in front of them, gaze at them a last time altogether, and thank them from the bottom of my heart.

— 11 —

THE ROMANCE OF CLOTHES

It is only once the collection has been completed and shown, that its life really starts in earnest. Those whose task it is to guide a dress on its first steps along the path towards commercial success, will think of me as a very unnatural father, because once the opening of the collection is over, I lose interest in my children, and practically never see them again.

For they have now ceased to be my children, and become objects of commercial value; the very evening of the day when they are shown to the Press, they are paraded in front of the professional buyers.

The first to come are the representatives of the big American stores, escorted by a representative of their Paris branch. They are as interested in precedence as the fashion-writers were. They have also paid a high price for their seats, or, to be more precise, they have paid a large deposit, as a safeguard, against the possibility that they will not buy anything at the show. Mme Luling and Mme Minassian have to pay as much attention to the hierarchical seating of the room, as the *Service de la Presse* did in the morning. New York and Chicago pair off. San Francisco is enthroned beneath a canopy. Boston faces the window, and shares a whole row of armchairs with Montreal. Each one has to be given the feeling that she, and she alone, is our most valued client. And alas, once again five people must be squashed in where only two were expected. The little *salon*, which the journalists scorned in the morning, now becomes the most prized situation, because fewer people can get in there and it is therefore less strictly supervised. To please our customers, we should have to litter the rooms with screens, behind which they would be able to watch the show without being watched.

The relative position of the various buyers in the *salon* depends above all on the importance of their respective shops, and these fluctuate to a certain extent with the activity of the firm. Mme Minassian will tell you with a smile that she has given a particular client a less good seat than she had at the last collection.

'I am punishing her, because she did not buy so much at the spring collection.'

The first visitors arrive at about three. They all know each other and we all know them. With the years, we have become a kind of little family. But these are hardened professionals and there is no time for idle chit-chat. Everyone keeps a poker face, their emotions well under control. Nobody wants to give away the fact that they like a particular model: on the contrary they do their best not to betray their preference to their vigilant colleagues. This makes the *placement* all important – and Mme Luling has given herself a migraine in her anxiety not to annoy anyone or favour anyone unduly.

The mannequins, who were received with rapture in the morning, now find themselves greeted with deliberate indifference, a perfect illustration of the rapid change of atmosphere which makes up a model's life. No longer an object of admiration for the connoisseurs, the dress has become a possible weapon in a competitive world. The girls, still elated with their recent glory, are always a little put out by this apparently dense reception. They still do their utmost to elicit applause, although the only models which stand a chance of receiving it are the ball dresses, which win the outward marks of approval deliberately held back from the day dresses, just because they are rarely ordered by the big stores.

Although I cannot hope to arouse delirious enthusiasm from this assembly of hard-headed experts (the scattered applause is never directed at the models which the applauders themselves intend to choose) I do look out for a certain quality of silence. The deeper and longer it is, the more I am sure that the model has been a success. The buyers are preoccupied with the smallest details of the collection, and the most honourable buyers who would react violently to the suggestion that they should copy a model they had not bought, seek – quite naturally – to augment their actual buys with detailed memories of the other dresses which they have not ordered. From this springs the rigidity of their attitude, a mixture of concentration and determination to give nothing away.

When Claire returns to the dressing-room, conversation breaks out in the *salon*. No one can prevent themselves altogether from commenting on what they have just seen and the buyers are eager to get hold of their particular *vendeuse*, in order to place a definite order. Certain buyers are conscientious enough to see the collection twice: others have no choice but to place an order that very evening. The most pressed are those who, like the Canadians, are leaving for their own country by aeroplane the next day.

Poor dresses! What a fate is theirs. As the right to buy includes that of examining the dress thoroughly, the models are now probed minutely for hours, measured, turned inside out, unstitched, sometimes literally pulled to pieces, in order that they may yield up their secrets. We are lucky if buttons and embroideries are not torn off as samples or souvenirs. During the slaughter, I prefer not to enter the *salons*, in order to spare myself the spectacle which would upset me almost as much as it upsets the dresses.

The *Service de la Presse* are demanding the dresses for photographs, Mme Minassian wants them for an impatient client, a *vendeuse* is asking to be given a particular dress, meanwhile a workroom is calling for the same dress in order to fit a customer. Of course they all want the same dress at the same moment, and all of them say it will only be for 'five minutes'.

When it is all over, which is often very late, Mme Luling, eternally gay and good-humoured and apparently never tired, actually has the strength to go out on the town with cousins in the fashion world, come from the four corners of the globe, who are delighted, after their working day, to rediscover 'gay Paree'.

The next day is the turn of the manufacturers. As many of the representatives of the big stores come twice, the confusion is if possible even greater than it was on the previous day. Behind each door, each screen, on every step, are sitting two people deep in animated talk: one is selling and the other is buying. One wanders and stumbles through the corridors in search of a model which remains obstinately unfindable. The excitement continues until the evening. The rational passer-by, who, late at night, sees the windows of the avenue Montaigne and the rue François 1er brilliantly lit, has no idea of the crafty follies which are going on behind the calm exterior.

Towards evening the *vendeuses* are exhausted and the clients at the end of their tether. If the session went on much longer, we should have to provide a picnic for them. As it is, there is champagne and whisky to revive flagging spirits. And the whirligig goes on. Each buyer has her own personal preference: she likes a particular *salon*, a particular mannequin; she also has her tiresome eccentricities, and she has her little jokes. Mme Luling manages to be everywhere at once in this chaos. She can put a name to every face and greet even the most forbidding expression with a smile. She looks sublimely unvigilant, but she is careful to see that no one takes a jewel off a model in a corner, or takes advantage of a dark nook to dismantle a whole dress.

Buying is a difficult art. The buyer has to know how to reconcile the needs of her clients with the desire for novelty, and choose the exact models which her particular *clientèle* will want from the hundred and seventy before her. Her choice is made at the cost of a great deal of hesitation, contradiction, and indecision. In the early hours of the morning, dead with exhaustion, the *vendeuses* go to sleep, convinced that all their clients are at one and the same time in a fearful hurry, and absolutely incapable of making up their minds. The next morning, fortified by sleep, they find that after all they are all charming.

Now it is the turn of Europe and the UN. A further row of chairs is added, the *placement* is arranged all over again, and the space in which the mannequins can revolve shrinks still further. This time buyers from all over the world are here to see the show. A *vendeuse* utters a protest in the cause of 'fifty Italians', whom she wants given good seats, another complains that 'her Montenegrans' have been tucked away in an insignificant corner. In the *salon* conversations are being held in every conceivable European language. Personally I have never wished to be present at this extraordinary show, in the course of which my dresses are treated like girls in a slave market, although I am aware that the public honours me by its appreciation!

As a general rule, the models which I personally believe to be promising disconcert the public at first, because their eye needs to get used to them. Dresses which proclaim novelty at any price put up the audience's backs when they are first shown. I have been regularly and successively insulted for showing first long dresses, then short dresses, then pigeon-breasts, then flat bosoms; for designing a tight waist, and for calling for a looser waist ... These contradictory criticisms generally emanate from the same pens.

For the next five months after the opening, the collection will be shown daily. After the foreign buyers come the Parisians themselves, then our international *clientèle*, finally, the simple tourists, for whom a visit to Paris includes a glimpse at the Dior collection. The star mannequins are by now worn out and only show the dresses during the actual show. Stand-ins are employed in order to show the dresses to the numerous clients who want to see the models again once the show is over, while they hesitate over buying them.

During all this time the drama – or should I call it the tragi-comedy? – of the copyists is being enacted in the various bars and hotels in the district round the avenue Montaigne. Despite the strict laws and the supervision exercised by each house, *haute couture* has not yet succeeded completely in keeping parasites and cheats from its doors.

There are five classical methods by which dresses are copied, of which the most distasteful is naturally that which originates with the treachery of a member of the staff. In view of the corporate nature of every collection, representing as it does the united efforts of *patron*, *premières*, workers, and mannequins, who have all staked their future with the success or failure of the show, this sort of betrayal is peculiarly odious. Every precaution is taken against it. The models, when they are carried from one part of the building to another, are either covered with a coat, or draped in white *toile* – so that the girls look as if they are carrying ghosts around. The sketches are carefully numbered; the *toiles* and models which have been rejected and which might indicate the general trend of the collection, are carefully shut up until the actual day of the opening. At the warning that a stranger is approaching, thick curtains are thrown over all the materials, hats, and trimmings in the studio. In every workroom, in the corridors even, there are numerous notices to remind the staff that 'Copying is stealing' and that 'Piracy kills our livelihood'. Personally I am glad to say that I have come across very few cases of this nature, and they all occurred in the few months following the opening of the firm.

The second method of copying takes place at a much later stage when the collection is shown to the Press. In most cases, what takes place is really a regrettable abuse of the details of the collection which are released, rather than proper copying. All the French journalists have to sign a special guarantee in front of the *Chambre Syndicale de la Couture,* before being given their special Press pass which admits them to the collections. They understand the extent of their rights: but some of their foreign colleagues, less sure, overstep the limits of good faith.

We have, dotted about the *salons,* three or four people whose sole mission is to discover these lapses: thus involuntary frauds are speedily uncovered. The miscreants are politely asked to hand over the sketches which they have made to us. The law of *haute couture* is implacable: 'Write all you like, but don't draw!' A rarer, but more serious occurrence is a deliberate attempt at copying. We unmasked one such scoundrel taking microscopic photographs, with a camera scarcely larger than a button. He was very quickly shown the door.

The third method of copying, and probably the most common, is the work of our clients, who thus show little regard for the rules of the profession. They sketch secretly some of the models which have been shown to them, pretending that they are trying to memorize the general look of a dress, whose name they did not catch. When they are discovered, we either make them buy the disputed model, or confiscate their sketches and keep their caution money. Into the same class fall the agreements which some foreign buyers reach with each other. They each agree to buy one particular model, then put all their acquisitions together so that they have a miniature collection assembled for a very small cost per head. This is more of a dubious extension of their rights as buyers, than an outright fraud.

This is how the secret of the new collection, at first only known to the creator and his immediate entourage, evaporates from showing to showing. If the new line is diffused too widely, too quickly, the collection loses much of its novelty, and therefore also its commercial value. This is the point of view of many of our clients who deplore the mass of photographs published in the newspapers, before their own dresses have been delivered. This influence of the magazine on the *couturier* is essentially different in Europe and America. In the U.S.A. the Press is treated as an accomplice in the world of fashion, whereas in France it is either ignored or feared. The French *couturier* tends to blame the Press for indiscretions and bringing down the value of the models. In my opinion he is wrong to do so because the picture of a dress in a magazine can inspire a woman to buy it, and whatever the skill and accuracy of a drawing or photograph, nothing can compare with the model itself. Without the *toile*, one is condemned to wear 'almost-the-real thing', which to the elegant woman is the same as 'nowhere-near-like' it.

The forms of fraud which I have just enumerated belong in the category of reprehensible activities: the two I shall now describe are systematic pillage, and constitute a grave prejudice to the future of *haute couture*.

The 'model renters' had their heyday in the years just after the war, and it was not until 1948 that their ringleader, a particularly cunning woman, was detected. She had bought through several intermediaries – generally private clients – the best models from the great Parisian *couture* houses. On her return to New York, she organized a miniature show of her own. This semi-official showing took place in the Plaza and admission was by invitation only. Every guest had to pay for his or her entrance to the tune of 350 or 500 dollars. For this price he had the right to take away any model he chose and return it three days later, after having carefully copied it. If he wanted to hire a larger number of dresses, he paid proportionately more; people even had to book certain specially popular dresses in order to have their turn at copying them.

In 1948, a preliminary warning cost the 'model renter' several million francs in fines to the *Chambre Syndicale le la Couture* – nevertheless she persisted in her trade, which was perfectly legal by American law. She came to an arrangement with several manufacturers who bought models for the stipulated price and augmented her New York collection. For three seasons French *couture* tried to protect itself by making secret marks between the lining and the material of each dress. As every buyer signed a formal agreement not to hand over any model for the profit of another member of the trade, it was necessary to discover the guilty people at this end of the chain in order to unmask the organization. A delegate of the *Chambre Syndicale* was sent to each show at the Plaza. Passing himself off as a client, he hired several dresses, unstitched an agreed corner of the lining, and wired off the numbers to Paris. Thus, little by little, all the manufacturers employed by the 'model renter' were discovered. It was also found that several of the models had reached New York via Rome, where the buyer, doubly attentive to his own interests, copied them overnight before sending them to New York by air.

In the course of this fight against fraud, a method of marking dresses was used which had been employed by the big laundries. It is based upon the use of an indelible ink, invisible to the naked eye, and only shows when the material is put under an ultra-violet ray. No dress now leaves my house without possessing this distinctive mark.

The 'model renter' was succeeded by the publisher of albums of sketches. The prosperity of this form of fraud – the most widespread which has ever been practised – is partly explained by the difference in legislation between France and America – the laws of the latter country being much looser as regards the artistic reproduction of commercial property.

Immediately after the opening of the French collections, even before the dresses have been delivered to our regular clients, a large number of subscribers receive at their homes, against a payment of a thousand dollars (the equivalent of our own caution money) an album of sketches containing the models of each leading house. If the buyer wants further albums, he pays proportionately more. He now has at his disposal a mass of documentation on the subject of the Paris collection without ever moving out of America, and the editor has the effrontery to demand his silence, under pain of prosecution!

In August 1955 alone, more than a thousand subscribers procured about three hundred models from the collections of the principal French *couturiers* by this means: 142 of my own models figured in the album, of which fifty-seven were exact copies. Half legally, half clandestinely, he recruited his manufacturers by word of mouth, and even extended his service to certain other countries in Europe, such as Switzerland, Germany, and Belgium. This miscreant has at last been unmasked and is now being prosecuted by a number of *couturiers*. What will become of him? The question is of real importance for the future of *couture*.

Who furnishes the editors of these albums with their information? I am afraid their informants are trusted guests whom we receive during the first days of the collection, perhaps even at the opening itself, since the sketches appear, at the latest, four days after the opening. By comparing notes with the various houses, it is possible to find out whose presence tends to coincide with pirating, but so far we have not been able to transform these suspicions into certainties.

The forgers must be exceptionally gifted. I have stated that 57 out of 142 of the models of my winter collection were reproduced exactly, although the copiers must have relied chiefly upon memory. It would be impossible for them to sketch in the essentials of a new line unknown to their neighbours, and the supervisors posted in the *salon*. Of course the programme with which all the guests are provided jogs their failing memories, but the annoying standard of accuracy points to exceptional powers of observation.

Quite apart from the grave financial prejudice caused by such practices, it is disagreeable to think that you have opened your doors, and perhaps your arms, twice a year, to one or several people who have come to see your collection with the avowed intention of robbing you.

Not having the soul of a Sherlock Holmes, or a Maigret, I have not sought to penetrate this distasteful mystery any further. In fact I have taken little part in the events which I have just described. Once the two opening shows are over, I do not linger long in Paris.

At the end of an uninterrupted work effort lasting six weeks, I have only one idea – to go back to the peace of my house at Montauroux. To me peace and quiet are a necessity of life. If I am in one sense a very busy man, in another sense I am a very lazy one. The application and care which I devote to my work are rooted in my desire to be finished with it as soon as possible. Fortunately I am innately conscientious, and therefore never stop until I am altogether satisfied with my work.

Three or four days after the opening of the season, I am off. It is not until I am actually in the train or the car that I feel really free. But the moment that I get to Montauroux, I feel the need of renewing contact with the avenue Montaigne. Every evening the telephone gives me news of what has happened during the day. I am told how the foreign buyers have reacted, what our best clients have ordered, and the principal cuttings from the Press are read out to me. In addition the graph of the sales is described to me. It begins to take shape from the first week onwards: the third day with timidity, the fifth with more assurance, and by the tenth its shape is clearly visible. It is rare that this initial indication is not confirmed in the weeks that follow.

As the days slip by, these telephone calls, which at first I await so passionately, begin to drop off; finally they cease altogether. Henceforth, from my point of view, the collection is definitely finished.

PART THREE

INSIDE A COUTURE HOUSE

— 12 —

THE MANNEQUINS

The dressing-room, or *cabine*, of the mannequins is a world of its own. Like a box at the theatre, it has its armchairs, its lamps, and its mirrors, and it has the same tawdry quality.

The mannequins or '*jeunes filles*' are obsessed by one idea – to look beautiful. Of course, they are all beautiful to start with, but at the same time they are all a little unsure of their own charms. Once they have finished their make-up, they turn to Mme de Turckheim who rules the *cabine* and ask her anxiously:

'Do I look pretty, *baronne*?'

If you fail to reassure them, they are thoroughly cast down, for at least five minutes – the time it takes them to correct their appearance in front of the mirror. Nowhere else would you find such a pure cult of beauty. The actress in her dressing-room is thinking of her part as much as of her face. The mannequin on the other hand is concentrated entirely on looking beautiful.

Chronically unpunctual, your mannequin bursts into the *cabine* exclaiming anxiously:

'I'm not late, am I?'

But if she is unpunctual, she can also move very fast. In the twinkling of an eye, she has undressed, donned a white overall, and sat herself down in front of her dressing-table. This forms part of a line, like a row of desks in a schoolroom; the *cabine* often reminds me of a class with its pupils studying to take a degree in beauty. In every desk is hidden a veritable horde of sweets, knitting, mascots, photographs, and *billets doux*. Each one of the mannequins has her own dressing-table, which she clings to. Renée for example would not surrender her place facing the door for worlds.

One night she dreamt that her place had been moved, woke up in floods of tears, and arrived at the *cabine* extra early next morning in order to reassure herself. All the mannequins are like Renée – creatures of fixed habits moving in a universe of hard work which engulfs them, and compels them to spend several hours every day at their mirror.

Mme de Turckheim, 'Tutu' to me and my staff, is always '*la baronne*' to her girls. She calls them '*mes filles*' whereas to us they are '*les jeunes filles*'. The administration and the workrooms call them more formally 'the mannequins'.

This little world bears no resemblance to the lurid pictures which have been painted of it, along the lines of the Edwardian chorus girls' dressing-rooms. Gentlemen in opera cloaks do not wait under the porches of *couture* houses, to take the mannequins' arms and guide them into waiting gilded carriages which will bear them towards slightly less gilded adventures. Today, it is the girls' husbands – if anybody – who wait for them, grumbling slightly because they are late. Most of them leave alone, in a hurry, and leap into a taxi or down the metro in order to get home as fast as possible. The lucky ones possess a good middle-class Simca car.

There is always a tendency in the public mind to invest the career of these girls with a false glamour which is very far from reality. They lead the sort of life which suits them, and they make the marriages which they want. The husband they are looking for is not necessarily Prince Charming or a millionaire banker, but a man whom they like, to whom they will be a loving wife, a good housewife, and an excellent mother. It is in order to lead this exemplary life twenty-one hours a day that they consent to lead the life of a butterfly for three. Ordinarily the mannequin spends from three to eight years in a *couture* house, battling with the exhausting existence of the shows and Press photographs, and then disappears.

Before speaking of the girls who are at present working for me, I should like to describe three of my former star mannequins whose lives have since developed in a different direction. For some of my '*jeunes filles*' I have a peculiar fondness, seeing them as Pygmalion saw Galatea. They alone can bring my clothes to life. In creating them even, I have had these girls in mind. It is not until they put on the model that I see the dress in its full glory. It is true that I am demanding: but who is not, in pursuit of the realization of his dreams?

Among the many mannequins I have known, one of the most naturally gifted was Tania. When I first knew her she was showing at Lucien Lelong, and was only sixteen. In several days she had acquired all the tricks of the profession, and had developed an entirely personal manner of showing clothes from her very first rehearsal. Tania shares with Praline, another mannequin I knew at Lelong, the quality of being a mannequin turned into a woman, rather than a woman turned mannequin. You have probably guessed that she is a Slav, and that is as characteristic of her as the fact that she is a mannequin. Her charm, her slightly less charming tempers, her contradictions, her extravagances are all Slav – but they have not stopped her leading the sort of life she wants. She has opened her own fashion house in Italy and, true to her temperament, has already lived through a thousand disasters and a thousand triumphs. Tania is femininity itself, with her ruses, her fibs, her little scenes, and also her grace, her sweetness, and her loyalties.

The greatest mannequin I have ever had is France. She realized perfectly my ideal: first of all by her figure, then by her slimness and blonde colouring. She looked particularly wonderful in seductive dresses, and when I took my collections abroad I loved to give her numbers to wear called 'France' and 'Paris', which were always applauded sensationally, with cries of:

'How beautiful she looks!'

She is so typically French, Parisian French, that I always think that in admiring her beauty, people are also admiring my country. For all her apparent guilelessness, she has achieved the sort of life she wanted: she now lives, happily married to a wealthy husband, beneath the easeful, voluptuous skies of the tropics.

Sylvie I took on when she was still scarcely more than a child, and throughout the whole of her career as a mannequin she remained the incarnation of the *jeune fille*. She wore the simple, unadorned, gay little models which young girls love. Her sparkling brunette appearance and her tiny waist suited these dresses to perfection. On the day of her marriage, however, she abandoned modelling forever, as if married happiness would henceforth prevent her from enacting the role of a young girl. What more charming example could there be of love of her profession, and respect for her role in it?

How can I best introduce you into the *cabine*? Let us say that it is five o'clock and the collection has just been shown. For an hour more, the mannequins still have to be ready to show a particular dress to a client, which she may have noticed during the show. So here they all are, waiting.

Odile, slight, fragile, and made still more distant and unapproachable-looking by her extreme short sight, is sitting at her dressing-table; she is thinking up complicated menus for her husband, who adores food. Catherine, still slenderer than Odile, if possible, is cutting a cake carefully into segments to share out among the other girls.

'If you're good, you'll get a bit!'

Lia, imperturbably Roumanian even in Paris, is telling a long story about how she has at last found herself a flat, and has burned her first joint. Victoire chooses this precise moment to enter with a *marron* pudding, which is submitted to the critical judgement of the other girls. Suggestions are many and various.

'If I were you, I would add a little vanilla.'

'And *lots* of cream.'

It's teatime, and all the girls are as greedy as kittens. One more legend by the board! The *cabine* of a fashion house is the negation of all the diet schemes which were ever invented. I hate to confess it, since it tells against me: but the truth is, that several hours a day of walking up and down with the quick thoroughbred steps of the mannequin is worth all the gymnastic exercises in the world, and is in itself enough to maintain a perfect figure.

Sweets are not the only subject of conversation in the dressing-room. Knitting, painting, philosophy, housework, the cinema, and the theatre are all discussed in turn. But the fact that my girls are not sirens, does not mean that they are a lot of shrinking violets: they are far from being prudish. Injected into their conversation are one or two stories, whose echoes even reach my studio!

If one of the mannequins is getting married or expecting a baby, the *cabine* is transferred into a workshop. Layette or trousseau, everyone wants to participate in a family event (in the sense that a *couture* house is a family). Scarcely a collection passes without one or other of these happy events taking place: and I am obliged to give leave of absence to a future mother, who is abandoning the A line or the H line for the Baby line.

After spending part of the day over-dressed and over-decorated, the girls are only too pleased to be able to slip into a mackintosh or fur jacket to go home, with a simple jersey and skirt underneath. It gives them a rest from the splendour and luxury with which they have to face the lights. The idea of the Model Cinderella who borrows one of the dresses from the collection to go, ephemeral and clandestine, to dance at a ball, is another fiction. In exceptional circumstances the mannequins can borrow one of the dresses they have worn, but they are never lent the dresses of the current season.

One by one, I have destroyed the myths which surround the profession of mannequin. Is all romance then fled from the profession? On the contrary, I believe that each age has its own special brand of romance, different but equally entrancing. The girls whom the journalists have christened the ambassadresses of elegance, certainly do not yield to their predecessors in glamour.

It is often put to me that my *cabine* of mannequins is run on rather different lines from that of other houses: it is probably true. As I am convinced that the good mannequin is born not made, I always interview every young girl who wants to get a job, wherever she comes from. It is true that there are specialized schools where girls can learn to walk, hold themselves, and act unselfconsciously. But the art of being a mannequin – it is the same in every artistic métier – can be subject to no fixed rules. One can generalize to the extent of saying that a mannequin ought to be tall and thin, but such impersonal standards have little value. A mannequin has to *be* – that is to say, have a separate existence as a mannequin; in addition her personality must correspond to the imagination of the *couturier*, so that she fits into the pattern of his creation.

Naturally every *cabine* employs a variety of different types of girls, because their clients will be of many different feminine types. But in spite of these differences, the girls have to share a common style, a sort of family likeness, characteristic of the house in which they work.

In order to become a mannequin, one has first of all to be able to walk, which is not easy. Many actresses, and even dancers, have come to see me, and to their great astonishment have been rejected. A natural and elegant appearance, and good deportment, all add up to that word which has rather gone out of fashion – *bearing*. Like successful dresses, born mannequins are elegant without effort. On them clothes spring to life and create their maximum effect. Above all, this effect is not achieved by artificial airs and graces, nor a sort of brazen smartness, designed to attract attention: the contemporary elegance is at once simple and natural.

Of all my mannequins, Renée is probably the one who comes nearest to my ideal. Every dress she puts on seems to be a success, as though there existed an exact equivalence between her proportions and those of my imagination. She brings fabrics to life so exquisitely that her face is lost. As she shows her clothes, distant, aloof, it seems as if her very life centres round the folds of the material.

Hieratic, and always a little mysterious, a mannequin must always succeed in gripping her audience. The theatrical expression 'to have presence', often misused, is exactly suitable here. It was for her 'presence' that I engaged Alla. She came one day with a friend, to apply for a job as a stand-in. As soon as I saw her, I begged Mme de Turckheim to take her on. There is a sort of panache about showing clothes destined for Western women, on such a deliberately Asiatic beauty. But Alla, for all the mysterious allure of the East in her features, is in fact half Russian. Her body is completely European, and the woman who chooses one of the dresses she has modelled will never find herself deluded. Alla is one of the born mannequins I have described. She was engaged on one day, and ready to show the collection on the next. She shows clothes with that aloof and impassive air which we associate with the East, but which she manages to combine with the natural fire and spontaneity of her Slav blood. Alla also speaks every language without an accent, as if she had been brought up in many different corners of the world.

I have never heard such a storm of criticism directed at a mannequin as that which greeted the arrival of Victoire. She came into my office practically on the eve of the collection. None of my staff thought she had the least chance of being engaged. They thought she was too small and, above all, that she did not know how to walk. It was quite true. But in spite of her dissimilarity to the other girls, I decided to engage her. She had a sort of look of Student Paris which I liked. I promised to make one or two dresses for her, and then, as fittings wore on, I realized that she was becoming one of my star-mannequins.

But I had jumped too far ahead of the taste of my public. At the sight of this newcomer, the Press and my clients combined to raise a chorus of protest:

'How dare you show a mannequin looking like that? What clothes! And what awful style! She isn't even good-looking.'

Some of my critics even went so far as to pretend that her presence in the show constituted an insult to my *clientèle*. In fact, I was fired at from all sides. But as I knew perfectly well that Victoire was delightful and had a feeling for her work, I stuck to my guns. When all the world was begging me to get rid of her, I decided to let her show a second collection. Suddenly, she was all the rage! Eyes were suddenly opened to her attractions. Her only crime had been that she epitomized exactly the youth of the time, and she was not very tall. People pretended that I had mysteriously transformed her, but in fact it was they who had changed, not she. All at once the angular charm of Victoire was apparent to them; henceforth she could do no wrong. Victoire became a star – and justified the triumphant christian name which I had given her.

Lucky, equally celebrated, is such a good mannequin that she did not choose her profession because she was pretty, but made herself pretty in order to fit herself for her profession. She comes from Brittany, and has the high cheekbones and slanting eyes which her compatriots, by some curious twist of fate, seem to have inherited from Mongolia. Every entrance is for her a matter of intense concentration: studying and interpreting the slightest nuance of a dress, she does not merely wear it, she positively acts it.

I wish I could describe all the mannequins under my roof. Together with the *premières*, they are my most important assistants. Their role may seem a passive one, until you remember that the most beautiful dress in the world can fail utterly and irredeemably if it is worn by a bad mannequin. This profession, which was once rather descried, has now become so popular, that parents encourage their daughters to go in for it, like the theatre. They even come to me themselves and beg me to engage their daughters. For every ravishing girl whom I interview, I have to see twenty who are obviously ill suited to such a career. All parents seem to be blind when it is a question of judging the beauty of their offspring.

The month which precedes each of the two yearly collections is an endurance test for the girls. From ten in the morning until eight at night, or sometimes as late as midnight, they are on their feet. They scarcely have time to go to the canteen to snatch a hasty lunch. I am always amazed by the stamina which these frail girls show. Nothing seems to break down their endurance. As Renée once said:

'The only thing which would stop us would be if we actually fainted away. But I don't believe that will ever happen to me!'

Stoically, they endure everything, and must surely be at the end of their strength by the eve of the battle. The *premières* are so obsessed by putting the last finishing touches on their dresses, that they completely forget that they are working on a human being, not a dummy. I often have to bring them back to reality, when I see the mannequin reeling with exhaustion.

'Hurry up! Let her go as soon as possible.'

The girl shoots me a grateful glance, but she says nothing. Just as the *première* is absorbed by the need to make her dress perfect, the mannequin is thinking of whether she will be beautiful and fresh for the morrow. She trembles with impatience when a last-minute hitch with a trimming threatens to prolong the session. The rest-room, which is near the studio, becomes a sort of dormitory where, on deckchairs, even on the floor, the mannequins sleep, eat, smoke, or gossip as they await the final fitting.

But the next morning, when Mme de Turckheim, entering the *cabine*, asks the ritual question – 'Everything all right, girls?' – they are there ready. All traces of the fatigue of the evening before have been miraculously effaced, as if by some magic formula. With only a few hours' sleep, they have gained fresh energy, and are as beautiful as goddesses. They sit, even more seriously than usual, applying their make-up. It is a sort of selfless concentration: they are making themselves beautiful for the sake of dresses they will wear, not for their own sakes.

The *premières* interrupt once more, with admonishments for the mannequin to take care over the beloved dress.

'Don't sit down, you're giving me a heart attack!'

'Don't make another move else you will disarrange the drapery.'

To listen to them, you would think the mannequins were idols to be venerated, not creatures of flesh and blood. The *premières* talk about 'my dress' as the medieval craftsmen talked about 'my masterpiece'. They are not dressing a girl, not they, they are simply allowing a body to be put inside their dress.

The dressers, for their part, are equally jealous in defence of their particular mannequin. Only their two charges are beautiful, only *their* clothes look wonderful, only *they* deserve to wear them. The dressers act like fierce watch-dogs, and even commit robbery on behalf of their girls. If an earring, a pin, or a ribbon disappears from the box of their charge, they are all set to steal a replacement from her neighbour's box.

Once the preparations for the opening are over, the period of really hard work lasts about two weeks for the mannequin. The morning is devoted to photographs for the house itself or the magazines; in the afternoon there is the show; in the evening the girls, worn out, are replaced by stand-ins to show individual numbers to the buyers. After these fifteen hectic days, the mannequin only has to clock in at three o'clock in the afternoon to show the collection to the clients. That lasts until the following collection, including summer or winter-sports holidays.

Once or twice a year, my collection takes to the air. Mannequins are often called Ambassadresses of Fashion – and their profession certainly takes them to the four corners of the globe – my girls have been to Japan, South Africa, Greece, England, Scotland, Austria, Italy, and South America. As a rule the little army which invades a foreign country consists of eight mannequins and four dressers accompanied by either M. de Mausabré or M. Donati, of the *Service de la Presse*.

With the exception of Renée, who hates leaving Paris, and will never go anywhere by aeroplane (how I sympathize with her!) all the girls love going on a journey. But of course these trips are far from being leisurely holidays for them. Showing a collection entails so much preparation and hard work that the girls are generally more anxious to go to sleep than to go dancing. Another legend must be debunked – that of the nightclubs, parties, and rich admirers with which a model is supposed to be surrounded. They have to be positively forced to go out, cajoled into attending a dinner. Even curiosity about a strange country does not seem to stir them sufficiently to want to see the sights, to the despair of Mme de Turckheim.

The one constant passion they all share is their solicitude for their own particular dresses. This is amply illustrated when a dress has to be entrusted to a stand-in, owing to some change in the time-table. The 'owner' always indignantly complains that it has been ruined, and the corselet has been stretched! Oh, this corselet, what heartaches it causes. All the girls tug it in as far as they possibly can, and in order to avoid ugly incidents, Mme de Turckheim has to make sure that she gets stand-ins at least as thin as, if not thinner than, the regular girls.

Of course the girls have their caprices and fancies. I know that within the precincts of the house I am often accused of being too indulgent towards them.

I hear murmurs of 'Monsieur Dior and his precious mannequins'. The administration tends to think that I employ too many, or that I pay them too much; the *premières* think I give in to their slightest whim; the *vendeuses* sometimes exclaim that they are impossible. In the midst of all these criticisms I hold my peace. The existence of a real affinity between a *couturier* and his mannequins is so vital, that it is worth a few small sacrifices in order to achieve it.

— 13 —

THE CLIENTS

I have already described the dresses, the way they are made, the mannequins who show them, and the professional buyers who order them. Now it is time to describe the last comers in this long procession – the women who will finally wear them.

The first private customers come and see the collection when the last professional buyers have gone. They may even overlap a little. Mme Luling, the *directrice de ventes*, who looks after all the actual sales of the clothes, listens for the heavy tread of those whom she terms, with a mixture of sarcasm and affection, her 'darlings'. How can I best describe our clients? I have said earlier that it is my ambition to be classed as a good craftsman. The first and most elementary duty of the *couturier*, as of all business men, is to give the customers what they want. Their demands are limitless, and we ruin ourselves trying to satisfy them, but we must not forget that they have every right to make them, even to overstep the limits of our forbearance. With that in mind, let us watch the clients arrive.

With their arrival, the *salon* takes on quite a different air. Always full, overfull (25,000 people see the collection every season) it ceases to be a workshop, and becomes a place of entertainment. As *mondaine* and frivolous as any other feminine gathering, it is composed of an audience which looks while it does not listen. Conversation centres round holidays, the latest play, other collections, and the latest piece of scandal ... while the eyes are fixed on the collection.

Scarcely has Claire disappeared in her wedding dress before

the rows of chairs come to life with a loud buzz of conversation. The *vendeuses* hasten to confer with their particular customers.

'Would Madame like to decide straight away?'

No, she would prefer to come back a few days later and choose her clothes in the calmer atmosphere of the fitting-room. She may not be in a hurry – but fifty others are. A miracle has to take place to satisfy them all – the miracle of the multiplication of the dresses. The successful models have to be reproduced then and there like Japanese flowers in a glass of water. These are all needed for exactly the same time, and – since there is no patience where vanity is concerned – any client who is kept waiting considers it a personal affront.

As soon as the first client who has managed to get the disputed dress displayed before her shows signs of finishing with it, an army of *vendeuses* hovers round her, ready to snatch it, in order to carry it off to their own clients, who are threatening to leave 'because, really, nobody seems to be in the least anxious to show me anything!'

The fitting-rooms are the scene of many a storm in a teacup, quick to flare up, and quick to subside. Exclamations of enthusiasm float out from behind the grey curtains.

'How well it suits you! It's absolutely the right dress for you.'

'Goodness, how brown you have got.'

Of course every woman is determined to squeeze into the dress of her choice, regardless of the differences between her figure and that of the mannequin, and the *vendeuses* have to perform feats of diplomacy in order to dissuade them.

'Lia wears it in the show … she's appallingly thin this season.'

Poor Lia, who's never looked better in her life!

These minor irritations, these disputes, battles even, over the models, all this endless fuss over them proves one thing to me – they are in demand and therefore they are a success. Nothing in the world gives me more pleasure.

Mme Luling's eyes are everywhere; she hastily stubs out her cigarette in an ash-tray in order to rush to avert a tragedy. Four times in the course of her journey to the scene of action she forgets what she set out for, as four different crises waylay her *en route*. Once she does arrive in a fitting cubicle, peace is instantly restored. The client, for whom the perfect fur evening wrap is now mysteriously produced from nowhere, gazes happily into the glass. But meanwhile Mme Luling, always with a pleasant smile on her lips, has already darted off somewhere else. She knows all her real clients by name, and has an unerring and unrivalled eye for detecting fakes. She can tell you, after one glance round the big *salon*:

'The woman in the sixth chair from the mantelpiece, in the third row, has brought her own little dressmaker with her again. That's the third time she's done it. Really, it's too much. I shall have to speak to her about it.'

At the end of the show, as the *salon* empties, Mme Luling knows better than anyone how to cope with those so-called friends who have come to see the show without any intention of buying, but nevertheless think it necessary to say to her as they proceed down the staircase:

'Your dresses are really delightful.'

She can also deal charmingly with those who say openly in front of her:

'It's obvious that only his evening dresses are any good this season.'

The showing of a collection has become a social event at which it is smart to be present. It is a good excuse for friends who have secrets to confide in one another to meet; it is also somewhat misunderstood, to judge by the telephone calls which the publicity department receives, in which they are asked to 'reserve a table for the show this evening'.

But I am determined to offer my show freely to those who come simply to feast their eyes; and I have given instructions to my *vendeuses* never to harass those visitors (whom we nickname 'swallows') who have obviously come with no intention of ordering.

When I opened my house, I told M. Boussac that I only wanted to dress the most elegant women, from the most elegant ranks of society. I have watched the *clientèle* I desired, build up, little by little, by the most natural means. It is for them that I am working all the time: it is they who answered my appeal – luckily I did not have to make it too pressing.

As it is my invariable rule not to enter my *salons* and never to intervene directly in the running of the business, I see my clients but rarely. The most intimate friend who comes to 30 avenue Montaigne finds Maison Christian Dior, and not Christian Dior himself. It is far better that it should be this way. My friends are free to buy or not as they please, without a feeling of embarrassment.

In the same way, it is always best to leave a client at liberty to make her own decision, when she is obviously contemplating leaving us.

'When they hesitate, I always advise them to buy elsewhere,' says Mme Minassian, who reigns with Mme Luling in the *salons*. 'Remorse is better than regret.'

The unfaithful one will probably return several weeks later, enchanted by a suit which she has bought from one of my colleagues, and only delighted to choose a cocktail dress from us. Or she may have been disappointed, in which case she upbraids her *vendeuse*.

'It's all your fault. You should never have let me go anywhere else.'

She increases her purchases from us at the same time.

With perfect good humour and a tinge of irony, Mme Linzeler, who supervises all the fittings, tells me:

'The best bargain in the world is a successful dress. It brings happiness to the woman who wears it, and it is never too dear for the man who pays for it. The most expensive dress in the world is a dress which is a failure. It infuriates the woman who wears it and it is a burden to the man who pays for it. In addition, it practically always involves him in the purchase of a second dress – much dearer – which alone can blot out the memory of the first failure.'

On the whole our clients are very faithful to us, although sometimes they try and make us believe that they are not, in order to obtain more rapid delivery, or a keener price.

There are some delightful cases of feminine logic pushed to excess, which are always rather touching, for example the charming lady who had a whole collection of black suits shown to her, wiped away a furtive tear, and finally murmured, as she made her choice:

'It's such a pity that mourning is so *common* at funerals.'

Another lady watched the show morosely. Nothing seemed to please her. When it was over she conferred with her *vendeuse* in a low voice, and finally, with a testing glance at Mme Luling, announced:

'This year, as my husband is ruined, I shall only order ten dresses.'

The story of the Deaf Aid still makes everyone in the building laugh although it happened some years back; the *vendeuses* love to recall it. It happened over a new, but by no means young client, who had chosen several dresses, and was coming for her first fitting. She was a foreigner, on her way through Paris, who was living in a rented flat. Mme Luling asked the *vendeuse* to remind the client discreetly of the indispensable little formality of the payment. The girl came back a few minutes later, seemingly overcome with emotion.

'Madame,' she gasped. 'This is not the moment to talk to her about payment! There's been a disaster! She's just had her telephone cut off.'

With these dreadful words, she rushed away. In one awful moment of revelation, Mme Luling envisaged all the dresses in the wardrobe, the work which had already been done, the unpaid bill, and the wrath of the management! What could possibly be got out of a woman who couldn't even pay her telephone bill? Cursing the 'darling' who had recommended this undesirable client to her, she also cursed herself for her carelessness in not finding out more about the client beforehand. Resolutely she made for the fitting-room, where she found consternation reigning. The *vendeuse* was not there, but the *première* looked as if she had been struck by lightning. As for the client, her uneasy smile bore witness to her embarrassment. After a few conventional politenesses, Mme Luling took her courage in both hands and launched into the fateful subject:

'We are terribly sorry to hear that you have been having trouble, Madame ...'

A frozen smile from the client, but no answer.

'But what are we to do with your dresses?'

The client's smile looked still more frozen.

Mme Luling was just getting ready to conjure up the forces of justice and the mysterious threats of the law, when the *vendeuse* rushed in, followed by an electrician. The cut-off telephone was in fact no more than the wire of her Deaf Aid which a clumsy thrust of the scissors had snipped through. A quick inspection by the electrician and it was mended. The client all of a sudden seemed to resume her natural ease of manner, the *première* her assurance, and Mme Luling her presence of mind. Only the *vendeuse* guilty of the misunderstanding and the client, who had not heard a word of what Mme Luling was saying to her, were completely ignorant of what had happened.

Let me end by telling my favourite story about the disloyalty of a customer. She was unfaithful in her private life, as well as in her dressing, for she had two lovers, one of whom dressed her at Fath, and the other with me. The two lovers and the two *couturiers* were equally ignorant of each other's existence. One day this delightful edifice of deceit toppled to the ground. The woman entered the avenue Montaigne in a suit by Fath and on the arm of a different gentleman from the one who ordinarily accompanied her. It was only at the beginning of the fitting, when the woman was in the midst of taking off her skirt, that she realized her mistake. She hastily whipped out her diary and checked the date, the time, the name, and the dress. Then she burst out, without thinking:

'Mon Dieu, what a fool I am! I thought it was Friday.'

I shall make no other revelations about my clients, cruel or kind. For two reasons: first of all, I detest spiteful gossip. Secondly, I should have to choose among my clients the dearest, and also, to satisfy certain people, the best known. The very idea of such a selection is distasteful to me. Furthermore, like a doctor, the *couturier* is bound by professional secrecy. As the *vendeuses* say to their clients:

'We see you all naked.'

So let us drop back the grey curtains of the fitting-room and leave our clients to choose their clothes in peace.

— 14 —

DOMESTIC EXPANSION

It was in 1946 that I moved into 30 avenue Montaigne. This delightful house then had enough elegant rooms and *salons*, sufficient nooks and crannies to contain all eighty-five of us.

None of us could possibly have envisaged that the increasing need for expansion would make us first of all absorb the stables, which I have described earlier, then the building which was built above them, then No. 13 rue François 1er, then little by little 32 avenue Montaigne. At the beginning not only did I feel perfectly content within the simple confines of No. 30 avenue Montaigne, but I also feared that it might almost prove to be too big. At the same time, what with three workrooms, the six fitting-rooms, and the various departments of the administration it must be admitted that we were already a little cramped. In order to keep ourselves within its bounds, we had to construct in the entrance a little room, four metres square, ventilated by a grill. I still sometimes wonder how Mme Luling managed to squash into it her two helpers, her files, her card indexes, and her telephones. As for the visitors who ventured in – where on earth were they put?

A little beehive, that is what my house was when I presented my first collection. I have before me now the Press release which I prepared then. It was photo-copied on to a simple sheet of paper. I stressed two principal silhouettes – the Corolla and the figure S. These long skirts, emphasized waists, and tremendously feminine fashions were instantly baptized the New Look. In the autumn, this trend was emphasized still more. The corollas curved outwards and the skirts, becoming longer still, restored all its former mystery to the leg. Tottering on high heels, women rediscovered a sort of dancing step, a gliding walk, which accentuated the fullness of the dresses.

The New Look brought me a heavy mail. If one measures the popularity of a star by the fan mail she receives, then I ought to have been considered a celebrity indeed. Letters arrived by the thousand – mostly enthusiastic but sometimes indignant. A garage owner from Los Angeles wrote and told me that he had sworn to 'tear me apart' on his next visit to Paris. According to him, it was my fault that his wife looked like a stuffed doll of the time of the Civil War. However, it's an ill wind …

In spring 1948 came the 'Zig-zag' line, which gave the figure the animated look of a drawing. With winter, this tendency was confirmed by the 'Winged' line. The silhouette had achieved its peak of youth and flightiness. When I opened the year 1949 with the 'Trompe l'œil' line, the Press release had already spread to four pages, and I was explaining at length the principles on which my collection was founded.

'There are two principles on which the " Trompe l'œil" line is founded: one is to give the bust prominence and breadth, at the same time respecting the natural curve of the shoulders; the other principle leaves the body its natural line but gives fullness and indispensable movement to the skirts.'

From season to season, new maxims enriched my little address: the appearance of hats, shoes, and gloves, expressed the progress of the house in practical form. The 'Mid-century' collection which followed that winter was very expert: it was founded on a system of cutting, based on the internal geometry of the material. I have mentioned earlier the importance of the grain of the material: at this period, my models exploited it to the utmost.

The collection of spring 1950 saw the triumph of the vertical line, which put 'woman' at a premium among women. Busts were narrowly moulded, waists well nipped-in, and colours were clear like daylight. At the same time I wanted to pursue the enterprising trends of the last collection. Thanks to numerous pleats and seams, I underlined the quality of infinite pains which I was anxious to bring out, that quality of 'work done by fairy fingers' which characterizes Parisian *couture*. Six months later, the vertical became oblique, joining dignity to impudence. Other themes were exploited: the 'Laced-in' and 'Lily-of-the-Valley' line. As for the evening dresses, they expressed the desire for luxury, calm, happiness, and beauty, which was in the air. The oval finally succeeded the oblique, and finally I introduced the 'Long' line, which was the favourite of all my collections.

It was now autumn 1951, and there had been striking changes at the avenue Montaigne. Behind the first little house, whose exquisite proportions I would not spoil for the sake of an empire, rose up a huge building of nine floors – and eight workrooms – paralleled by another building also of eight floors, but with two workrooms on each floor. The administration, previously installed in the house in the rue François 1er, occupied one of these floors, then finally established itself in the covered court of the newly annexed building.

The building at 13 rue François 1er was first of all occupied by the Economic Ministry. It had to be won by a great battle: but eventually we succeeded in occupying a great part of it. But certain other offices, refractory at the sight of our insidious progression, proved to be irreducible. Finally a strike of protest on behalf of our workers, and the action of an understanding ministry delivered up to us the last pockets of resistance.

So Christian Dior Perfumes were installed on the first floor, and stockings on the second. On the third floor was established a studio corresponding in importance to the collection which I had to create. Above were three floors of workrooms, crowned on the seventh floor by a sickroom and a welfare department. As for the *boutique*, which had previously occupied several square feet, it had now literally exploded!

It is on St Catherine's day that you should really visit 30 avenue Montaigne. In our profession, this feast of our patron saint has a tremendous importance. For me, it counts a great deal. I visit all the various departments and in the little speech which I address to each workroom, I try to express the sincere and tender affection which unites me to all those who join their efforts with mine –

whatever their part, big or small – in order to achieve the success of our enterprise. On that day, in the welcome which is given me, in the decorations of the rooms, in the invention employed in the decorations and the costumes, I seem to lay my finger on the pulse of the whole building. There is nothing gayer than St Catherine's day. Each workroom has its own orchestra, and throughout all the buildings, there is one continuous ball.

Growing up in age and in size, Maison Christian Dior was making its way in the world. Since 1948 it had opened a house in New York, and concluded agreements with England, Canada, Cuba, Australia, Chile, and Mexico. It was becoming obvious that the peaceful little business which I had at first envisaged was in the process of devouring me. A referendum organized by the Gallup Poll chose this moment to give me the unexpected honour of saying I was among the five best known international personalities. Fashion, what excesses do we commit in your name!

1952 was a serious year from the first – the year when the Iron Curtain was heavily clamped down, fires were lit in Indo-China and Korea, and Arab nationalism was reviving … away with the euphoria of the New Look, and the fripperies of yesteryear. The new essential of fashion was that it should be discreet.

That is why in spring 1952 I proposed the 'Sinuous' line; to indicate that fashion, for once logical, was succeeding the rigours of winter with a season of suppleness. Blouses and sweaters became the major theme of the collection, whose colours oscillated between natural and grey. At the same time the waist became looser. The road towards the 'Arrow' line – which is the exact antithesis of the New Look – was opened up.

Evening dresses, to which two seasons earlier I had given the names of musicians, now bore the names of authors. This nomenclature caused some curious conversations in the workrooms. In the morning a client would be entranced by André Roussin, and in the evening she would telephone to say that after all, she would go all out for Jean Paul Sartre. The *vendeuses* complained that they could never lay their hands on Paul Claudel or François Mauriac.

In the *cabine* a mannequin would exclaim crossly:

'Look out! You're crushing Maurice Rostand,' or 'Don't trample on Albert Camus like that.' In her perennial role of the bride, Claire wore Beaumarchais, an allusion to the Marriage of Figaro.

I received one letter of protest. It was from an old gentleman, indignant that the name of his grandfather had been given to this 'nonsense which is supposed to be a dress'. Heaven knows what ill chance had guided me to exhume from the depths of a dictionary – where he slept in peace, bearded and completely forgotten – this particular ancient academician.

In the autumn the silhouette took inspiration from modern techniques with the 'Profile' line. The following spring, appeared the 'Tulip' line, marked by the development of the bust and the narrowing of the hips.

Little by little the waist was being freed. Colours were inspired by the pictures of the Impressionists, and evoked the fields of flowers dear to Renoir and Van Gogh.

It was in that year that an American journalist wrote to me challenging me to a duel, on the pretext that I was disfiguring the American female figure. To tell the truth, my adversary, by publishing our two photographs alongside each other, was aiming less at injuring me than at advancing himself.

Six months later, when I had just founded a branch at Caracas, I launched the 'Eiffel Tower' line and 'Cupola' line which were modelled on these two monuments of Paris. I was always searching to alter the general attraction of woman and enliven her silhouette. The material ought to live on her shoulders, and her figure live beneath the material. That year also, for the first time, the model girls wore shoes made by the newly founded firm of Christian Dior-Delman, created and directed by Roger Vivier.

In the spring of 1954 I put forward the 'Lily-of-the-Valley' line, inspired by my lucky flower, a line which was at once young, graceful, and simple, and which was given unity by its colour: Paris blue. Christian Dior now reached the age of reason and celebrated his seventh birthday. He now occupied five buildings, included twenty-eight workrooms, and employed more than a thousand persons. Eight firms and sixteen allied companies spread their tentacles over five continents.

The namesake which I had seen grow up at my side could feel well satisfied himself! His daily mail included letters from madmen, criminals, megalomaniacs, geniuses, called him in turn madman, a criminal, a megalomaniac, a genius, a grand vizier, an emperor, or a dictator of fashion, in letters or newspapers coming from Australia, Florida, Germany, Italy, or Japan. A lawyer from Texas wrote asking for a legionnaire's kepi with a white veil, and a woman living in Paris offered him her house for a ball 'under the presidency of the masked princess'.

'Why not dress your guests as the shades of the great lovers of the past?' she suggested.

From Alsace a woman who had lost everything, *Heimat, Habe, und Gut*, wrote asking to be dressed once by him before 'leaving this world'. She signed the letter 'A poor dreamer, who has done no wrong'. An Englishwoman, the wife of a conjurer, appealed to the similarity of the *couturier*'s profession to her husband's, to get an evening dress. An Italian *couturier* wrote on behalf of all dressmakers (*per tutti i sarti*) and asked for a contribution towards the placing of a statue of the Archangel Michael on Monte Sant' Angelo, *al patrone della categoria sarti*.

Let all my correspondents, from the highest to the lowest, rest assured that I never read any of their letters. My secretary receives huge baskets full of them and is instructed to open them without ever referring them to me. It is in fact she who has provided me with the few extracts which I have quoted above.

A line which was tremendously criticized, deformed, and abused, was my so-called 'Runner bean' line: and I think it as well to recall exactly what it did consist of. It was based on the length and flattening of the bust, and suggested the tapering figure of a young girl, like the nymphs of the famous Fontainebleau school of painting. Love of style, purity, reserve, and elegance character-ized this particular epoch of the Renaissance when the art of Jean Goujon flourished. The H line marked the final evolution begun in 1952 by the liberation of the waist.

The morning after the presentation of the H line, Carmel Snow cabled back to *Harper's Bazaar* in America: 'The H line represents an even more important development than the New Look.' Almost immediately the new line was baptized the 'Flat Look'; but it had never been my intention to create a flat fashion which would evoke the idea of a runner bean. Nevertheless, the idea, and the main points of the new fashion, were firmly launched, and there was nothing I could do to stop them. This time I got an indignant letter from a farmer in Idaho:

'With your so-called genius, you have succeeded in disfiguring my wife. What will you say if I go and send her over to you?'

The A line and Y line which succeeded the H line are still of too recent date for me to discuss them at length. In the spring of this year I put forward the 'Arrow' line which confirmed the tendencies begun by these two. Line by line, that is the history of my house.

— 15 —

PARIS TO NEW YORK AND BACK AGAIN

I have described earlier how I installed a *boutique* at the bottom of the staircase at 30 avenue Montaigne, with the help of my dear friend Carmen Corcuera, now the wife of François Baron, for which Christian Bérard suggested the decor. It was a sort of little portico entirely papered with cream *toile de Jouy*, covered in sepia drawings. Carmen spent whole days, perched on a ladder, draped in *toile de Jouy*, seeing to the details, and arranging the hatboxes which Bébé Berard had envisaged decorating this pocket-sized shop.

The *boutique* opened at the same time as my first collection. At first it only offered a choice of trinkets, such as jewels, flowers, and scarves, but it was not long before more ambitious projects were undertaken. In the summer of 1948, Carmen suggested that the *boutique* should also sell dresses, which while they adhered to the general line of the collection, would be simpler and less elaborate in execution. Her idea was received with such enthusiasm that 'the *boutique* collection' was born. Mme Linzeler, who had just joined us, looked after it, together with a fitter, Yvonne, and one assistant. Working like blacks in one corner of a workroom, they performed prodigies, while Carmen, whose *boutique* was already bursting out at the seams, was forced to go up one floor to the next landing.

At the same time, gloves, perfumes, stockings, and later, ties were introduced; the *boutique* experienced, quite independently of the main collection, the feeling of showing its wares to the gaze of the public. Each season it was entirely redecorated in the spirit of the big collection. It finally swallowed up the studio, which was allotted to it on the other side of the porch, set up its own studio and three workrooms, and soon had its own *clientèle*, quite separate from the *clientèle* above its head. Abounding with novelties of all sorts, including presents, for men as well as women, and even small pieces of furniture, it threatened to crack in half like a conjurer's egg, to reveal a plethora of coloured handkerchiefs.

Elaborate negotiations were set in motion with a bar, a tax-collector, and two shops, in order to get possession of the ground floor and first floor of the house in rue François 1er. In June 1955, the *boutique* closed one evening in 30 avenue Montaigne, and opened the next morning at 15 rue François 1er. This magic transformation took place during the night, under the direction of Marie-Hélène de Ganay, Carmen having finally resigned in order to get a little rest. In a few days Victor Grandpierre had created a *Louis XIV-Belle Époque boutique* which exactly corresponded to what I had imagined. Surrounded by assistants, and caught up in a whirlwind of *vendeuses* transporting the stock, he spent the whole night putting the finishing touches to the decor.

When I arrived the next morning, I found that where only the night before there had been a mass of paint and stepladders, there was now an exquisite and orderly *boutique*, which had somehow already managed to achieve the atmosphere of life and energy which I consider so vital to my house. There is nothing I detest more than a beautiful room deprived of the feeling of life: it is like a pretty woman who lacks charm. At half past nine in the morning the first client entered, and bought a coat, obviously without having the slightest idea of the transformation which had taken place during the night.

I wanted a woman to be able to leave the *boutique* dressed by it from head to foot, even carrying a present for her husband in her hand. The expansion which took place beneath my eyes, showed that my ambition was not far from being realized. All the activities which are now associated with my name, were to be found within the walls of the *boutique*: the stockings, gloves, and perfumes, whose rise to fame has been parallel to that of my house itself.

The public has little idea of the care and worry which goes into the search for a new perfume which they see simply in a little packet. It is such an absorbing occupation that today I feel myself as much a *parfumier* as a *couturier*. I must not conclude this little picture of my subsidiary activities without mentioning the *salon* where the Dior-Delman shoes are sold, under the direction of my friend Roger Vivier, who creates the most elegant shoes in the world.

While the *boutique* was undergoing these adventures, I was collecting together and sorting out in my own mind all the various impressions which I gathered from my first journey to the U.S.A. Like all Frenchmen, I had been struck by the amazing, stunning richness of the United States. Wastage there seemed not only natural but was actually recommended as an essential factor to the prosperity of the country. My upbringing made this philosophy a tremendous shock to me, but later the terrific creative energy of the Americans encouraged me towards further creative enterprises of my own.

But before I could venture out into this new field, I had to get to know the situation really well at first hand. At the end of the Second World War, the United States was not the luxury-deprived country which France and England, blitzed and bomb-damaged, still were. The continent of feudal millionaires which Boni de Castellane discovered, has practised democracy even in its elegance, creating thus a state of general material well-being still undreamt of in Soviet Russia. Thanks to mass-production, America has brought luxury within the means, if not of everyone, at least of the majority of its population.

In 1948, this was an important fact which I had to take into account. I had also had to take into account the almost prohibitive customs duties imposed by America, which although she preached commercial expansion, only expected herself to benefit, with the selfishness of a child who only plays to win. This one-sided notion of exchange prevented the arrival of the huge dress trade which had made the fortunes of Parisian *couturiers* between the two wars. Essentially a philanthropic nation, America has made the mistake of thinking of aid to other countries in terms of charity, innately distasteful to the pride of ancient countries like my own, rather than in terms of the free exercise of honourable commerce. This seems to me a short-sighted policy, although perhaps it is scarcely tactful for a Frenchman, whose own parliamentary government is the most striking example of political ineptitude, to say so.

To return from the general to the particular instance of *couture* : I realized that my Paris house would have to remain a laboratory, and its dresses the prototypes, destined for a luxury *clientèle* and the professional buyers. If I wanted to reach the numerous elegant Americans, for whom the annual journey to Paris was at present a semi-essential pilgrimage in the interests of *chic*, I would have to open a collateral house in New York. It would be called Christian Dior–New York to mark the difference between its models and those of the mother house in Paris. In other words, I intended to risk the crossing of the ocean and starting up a new venture in a foreign country.

A multitude of proposals were made for us to work – like certain of my colleagues – within the framework of an existing organization. But I wanted to remain independent, in order to preserve the dignity, distinction, and pre-eminence of Parisian *couture*. Also, as I was supposed to be opening an American house, it seemed sporting to run the same risks and put myself on an equal footing as an authentic American business.

I had to make two or three journeys to New York to launch my new project. A building and staff had to be found – in short a house had to be established, with all that implies in the way of negotiation and hard work. Fortunately, Mme Engel, who has since become the manager of Christian Dior–New York, appeared at that precise moment and played the role of guardian angel. Half Russian and half Swedish by birth, she combines the charm of the Slavs with the strength of character of the Scandinavians. She has been settled in America for a long time and knows it extremely well: but she also understood immediately my own problems as a Frenchman. In short she formed the ideal meeting point between the ideas of two continents. Her loyalty and warmth made up entirely for the strong-mindedness and impulsiveness – common to American women – which I might otherwise have found excessive. She was a wonderful guide for me in my researches into the American way of life.

After many doubts and delays, I ended by renting a place of truly American proportions, at the corner of Fifth Avenue and 57th Street right in the middle of the city. I could not bring myself to work on Seventh Avenue, where most of the big houses are, as I thought the 'ready-made' atmosphere would be demoralizing. But the most difficult problem still remained to be solved: that of choosing the staff and, most important, the *chef de production*. He is the keystone of the *couturier's* arch. It was essential that I should make a good choice, more especially because, despite my numerous inquiries, I was practically ignorant of the American market. Once this rare bird had been found, I was able to choose the manager of my *salon* and a *vendeuse*. As for the mannequins, they were relatively easy to find among the ravishing New York model girls, who had managed to protect their natural elegance from the effects of over-sophistication. I would not have dreamt of importing French girls, who would not have at all the desired style and whose proportions would have been all wrong for the American market.

All our preliminary steps took place in an encouraging atmosphere of hope and ease. America is the land where every new enterprise, every original idea, encounters the warmest welcome, and arouses the most lively interest. Nowhere else can the gap between the project and its realization be bridged so straightforwardly. The Americans know how to take a chance: they offer you generously the whole armoury of success. If things do not turn out right, it does not matter all that much, there is always another race to be run and there is absolutely no bitterness towards the horse that has failed. Fair play reigns completely in business. These are facts which a European, above all a Frenchman, used to distrust, parsimony, and unproductive talks, ought to acknowledge with gratitude.

Having once established the house on a sound business footing, I turned to my favourite preoccupation – the decoration of the interior. Even though he was not a professional, I begged my friend Nicolas de Gunzbourg to undertake it. His own background was proof enough that he was capable of creating the precise atmosphere, suggesting at once New York and Paris, which I wanted. He was kind enough to agree, and I sailed for France, entirely happy in my own mind about the future of my new enterprise. A rough date was fixed when the buildings would be ready to receive us, my staff and I, to prepare the first collection.

When we reached New York nothing was ready. Contrary to the widely held notion, Americans are not really people in a hurry. On the contrary they all seem on their honour to be late, particularly the contractors. In short, as our own buildings were not ready for us to work in, we had to fall back on what we could find. I decided to install myself temporarily in the little house on 62nd Street where we were living, Mme Marguerite, Mme Bricart, Mme Raymonde, and I. I turned the winter garden into a studio, the two drawing-rooms into workrooms, the pantry into an accounts department, and a bedroom into a dressing-room for the models. We tried to fit ourselves into the remaining rooms as best we could.

We were certainly camping. Thank heaven the owner of the house never had the bright idea of paying us a visit: she would have been absolutely horrified. Literally piled on top of one another, we ate while we had fittings, we slept beside the tables on which the material was being cut out, at every step we stumbled over the rolls of material, and never could remember, when we went to the pantry, whether we were supposed to be collecting napkins or a piece of material.

We all found this atmosphere very amusing, as we knew it was only temporary – not so the four lots of servants who came and went during the two and a half months of our occupation. None of them lasted longer in our service than the time they needed to give their week's notice. The first to go was an impeccable butler, an expert at handing round cocktails, but apparently at very little else. The indescribable untidiness of the house visibly moved him. When we presented him with the vacuum cleaner and the saucepans, and told him to get on with it, he could bear it no longer. Horrified, he left for bars more worthy of his talents. At the mere prospect of remaining alone in our tender care, the coloured woman we had engaged to help him instantly left without even asking for her wages.

A Swedish cook replaced them. Newly freed from the austerities and rationing of France, we were all eagerly looking forward to the Scandinavian specialities which we fondly imagined he was going to prepare for us. But apparently he was used to a grander set-up, more in keeping with his Viking's stature: he merely set fire to our doll's kitchen. Which done, he fled out into the street, insulting those who rushed to our rescue.

Next we opted for two old Irish women. They at least would know how to appreciate the charm of our charmingly bohemian *ménage* … At first our relations were idyllic, and the four of us spent whole evenings extolling the virtues of the Emerald Isle. Alas, the dream did not last! The two old girls came to see us together and jointly gave in their notice. Their modesty was affronted by the nakedness of the poor shy model girls.

This time we really thought we were lost. It was at this moment that heaven chose to send to our rescue a wonderful Frenchwoman, actually a lady of the streets, in search of an officially respectable profession; she was at the same time gay, reliable, and a wonderful cook and immediately set out to worship and spoil us. With outrageously blonde hair, but impeccable overall, our angel knew how to cook, how to sweep, and pampered us so much that we were at last free to look after our business cares.

All this time the workrooms were a source of ceaseless anxiety to us. Ignorant of our methods, our American recruits found it impossible to understand why we insisted on having five or six rehearsals of a finished dress. In the conviction that the successful reproduction of a good drawing would result in the production of a well-made dress, they put our meticulous labours down to stupidity or clumsiness. In their opinion only the worst of amateurs could possibly work with such care. Our care over perfection seemed absolutely inexcusable to them.

While I was battling with these, and a thousand other cares, I was suddenly landed with an unexpected major crisis. All at once, everything seemed to go wrong, and as a result of what follows, I suffered for years under the impression that America, the country which is supposed to be the champion of liberty, is in fact a monstrous tyranny.

In order to protect our clients against deformations and harmful copyists, we had, in Paris, made our buyers sign a contract engaging not to reproduce our models except under certain conditions. This attempt at safeguarding artistic production and a high standard of quality was obviously not agreeable to everyone, no more than the opening of our New York branch was. We suddenly found it to be a piece of administrative orange skin, on which our entire New York arrangements were slipping up.

I have a horror of lawyers and legal proceedings. So I was appalled one morning to receive a summons to come before the American Anti-Trust Department for an examination. I, whom the very sight of a uniform fills with a profound sensation of guilt, had to pass through the door of the Anti-Trust building, flanked by two lawyers – how much more ominous as well as more austere, than our own palaces of justice. I had to undergo a cross-examination of more than two hours, which even to this day I have never fully understood. My lost air, my obvious vagueness, saved me. I had no need to play a part. Incapable of discovering from me the slightest financial details of my affairs, my inquisitors soon saw that the wicked conspiracy which I was supposed to have entered into, in fact had no serious basis. The famous contract was annulled. But this episode reinforced my conviction, in which all the serious American *couturiers* concur, that the pillaging of artistic creation is not only authorized in the United States but also encouraged. Nothing effective can be undertaken in its defence.

Finally, in spite of all obstacles and pricks, the collection developed in the little house on 62nd Street was ready, while the decoration of the building on Fifth Avenue was nearly finished. So several days before the opening of the season, we were able to transfer workrooms and staff from one to the other. Nicolas de Gunzbourg had carried out my ideas to perfection.

As the date of the opening drew near, I was overcome with an even more intense attack of nerves than I ordinarily experienced in Paris. I was dealing with a public which was completely new to me. I had to remain both faithful to myself, and to adapt myself to very limited measurements, to different types of material, and to a much shorter show. I was anxious to know if I had succeeded.

On the appointed day, the atmosphere in the *salons* disconcerted me. Everything went on in a sort of calm and stolidity most unlike the fevered atmosphere at avenue Montaigne, which I found in some way demoralizing. The New York audience is much more relaxed, much more careful of its comfort and ease. Their *salons*, like their theatres, are immense by French standards. Everyone wants an armchair reserved in advance which will serve as a protection against the waves of assault, and will enable him to see everything without turning his head. The fresh atmosphere maintained by the air-conditioning prevents the body, and the spirit as well, from becoming overheated.

The applause which greeted the show was very different in calibre from the frenzy we were used to in Paris. The reserved air of the very same journalists whom I had seen watch our show with visible excitement in France worried me, until I read their pieces in the newspapers covering me with praises. This frigid appearance is an Anglo-Saxon phenomenon as the editor of a New York magazine once explained to me:

'If pleasure varies in its expression from one continent to another, that does not mean that it is any the less profound or sincere. In France you cry out, you kiss your neighbours to express your enthusiasm … In America, we are filled with the same exhilaration, only with us it is silent.'

With the years I have grown used to contrasts, so that today, now that my house has successfully established itself in New York, I feel that I am a genuine American *couturier* in New York, just as I feel I am a French *couturier* in Paris. Little by little, I have learnt how to understand the needs and wishes of the American *clientèle*. The heat, natural in the summer, and artificial in the winter, ought to be called 'tropical'. Nothing is ever thin, light, and fresh enough for them. The flats are relatively small, nightlife is intense, active, and conducted very much in public in clubs and other public places. There is a great demand for short evening dresses and rather formal restaurant dresses. But of course the real master-pieces of American design are the cocktail dresses, the cocktail being the symbol *par excellence* of the American way of life. For the daytime, a suit is the indispensable uniform, and the famous little black dress so dear to Parisians is very little worn.

On the whole the American women – with the exception of those who dress in France – attach less importance to the small details of fit and to the finish of a dress, than to the general effect of the whole outfit. They are attracted by variety and frequent change, and for this reason their streets are therefore much gayer than those in Europe where luxury lies behind closed doors. It must also be admitted that the high standard of life in the U.S.A. narrows the gap between the leisured and working classes. The Cadillac, a rather brash sight in Paris, there passes unnoticed in the midst of a crowd of other cars almost equally luxurious, belonging to office clerks or even lift boys. In the same way luxurious clothes have not the shocking, voluptuous effect they have with us.

Since we have deliberately crossed the Atlantic, let us now pass from the subject of one America to the other. Christian Dior–Caracas is a charming miniature reproduction of the Paris house. It bears witness to the brotherhood under the skin of all the Latin races. Throughout the length of my stay in Caracas, despite the exotic countryside, the exuberance of nature and people, the immense richness and taste for display, I never once felt myself far from home. When chance or necessity takes you far from your native land, how reassuring and comforting it is to rediscover its essential qualities and even its defects.

— 16 —

CHRISTIAN DIOR-LONDON

Because my London house is my last born, I am probably devoting more time to it at the moment than to any of my other houses. I am captivated by its novelty, of course, but it has another charm all of its own. To me it is part of England, England whose charms I first discovered in my twenty-first year.

It was in 1926. The hour of my enrolment in the army was approaching, and I persuaded my parents to allow me to spend several months in Great Britain to perfect myself in my study of the language, and spend my last months before my military service in this country which attracted me so much.

Was it because I was just twenty-one? Was it because I was, for the first time in my life, absolutely free? I felt myself far enough from my family to be independent and at the same time near enough to them to summon their aid, if need be. Or was it simply because in that year London was more beautiful than ever? Whatever the truth, I cherish an unforgettable memory of my visit.

The happy impressions of one's youth are always tenacious. Years later, revisiting a town seen in one's youth, one finds that these pleasant memories are still intact. Each of my subsequent visits to Great Britain has given me the same sensation of happiness and personal liberty which I experienced on this first visit. For one thing I love being in a country where the past lies so vividly around me. Once I became a *couturier*, I added to the pleasure of being tourist, that of dressing English women: for personally I find them among the most beautiful and distinguished women in the world. When an English woman is pretty, she is prettier than a woman of any other nationality. I adore the

English, dressed not only in the tweeds which suit them so well, but also in those flowing dresses, in subtle colours, which they have worn inimitably since the days of Gainsborough.

Before I set up my English house, I had already had two ravishing ambassadresses from London, in the shape of two English models. The first, called Dexter Vaughan, seemed to me a walking embodiment of beauty and majesty. When she was dressed in a ball dress she used to radiate such splendour that her dresser – after doing her up – used to sit down in order to gaze at her at leisure. Few models, few girls indeed, possess such a fresh and dazzling complexion as Dexter did: when she was near we felt we were in the presence of a nymph, newly bathed in a fountain, and we were all desolate when she left us to get married.

The next was Jean Dawnay, whom we christened 'Caroline', in order to avoid confusion with an American girl working for us at the same time, called Jane Burns. I chose 'Caroline' for her essential Englishness – she had blue eyes, golden hair, and a slender, graceful figure. I should also mention Diana Massie, an Australian girl who came to us as a mannequin, and switched over once she was within the avenue Montaigne, and is now one of our best *vendeuses*.

The world of English fashion itself was not unknown to me either. I had also had the honour of showing my own Paris collection in London, before I actually set up a separate English house. It was actually my second collection, in the autumn of 1947, and Mrs Doris Langley Moore, who has recently opened a delightful museum of costume, organized a sumptuous presentation at the Savoy. It took place on the Friday: and the next morning my staff and I found ourselves involved in something like a thriller plot. Through the good offices of Madame Massigli, wife of the French Ambassador in London, whose help and encouragement of French *couture* I can never sufficiently praise and acknowledge, it was arranged for us to show the dresses privately to H.M. the Queen, now the Queen Mother, Princess Margaret, the Duchess of Kent, and her sister Princess Olga of Yugoslavia. These ladies were all devoured with curiosity to see the 'New Look' dresses, of which they had heard so much.

As neither the police nor the Press had been warned, we all had to act with the greatest possible discretion, in order not to attract attention. The huge ball dresses, with their voluminous skirts concealed by covers, were smuggled out of the service door of the Savoy. The whole operation took place amidst a tell-tale rustle of material and constant hasty 'sshs'. Finally we all, mannequins, staff, and dresses arrived at the exquisite Embassy which Madame Massigli had done so much to make beautiful. We had one final, chaotic, rather emotional rehearsal there, in order to get used to the different length of floor. The mannequins were all taught how to reconcile royal protocol with the other strict protocol – that of the show.

I was told that the Queen would graciously exchange a few words with me once the show was over: and I may add that whatever the French may say, they are all fervent royalists at heart! Certainly I am. Face to face with the Queen, I was instantly struck by her elegance, which I had been quite unprepared for: that, and the atmosphere of graciousness which she radiates. The mauve dress and draped hat which she wore would have been quite inconceivable on anyone else – as it was, on her they looked wonderful, and I felt that nothing else would have shown her to such advantage. The grace which radiated from her and her smile were appreciated by all of us present.

Beside the Queen was Princess Margaret. At that time she crystallized the whole popular frantic interest in royalty. The public had chosen well. She was a real fairy princess, delicate, graceful, exquisite. I had heard that she was also extremely intelligent and witty, but her poise and the formality of the occasion prevented me from finding out for myself. Later, however, when she was in Paris, she honoured my *salon* with a visit, and I found that she was keenly interested in fashion, and also, unlike many women, knew exactly the sort of fashions which suited her fragile height and Titania-like figure.

To return to this little ceremony at the French Embassy – you can imagine that we walked on air back to the Savoy.

That very same afternoon, Norman Hartnell, the court dressmaker, came round to see me at the hotel. He had seen the show the day before, and told me that he thought my collection so pretty that in his opinion it was worthy of being shown to Her Majesty! Here was a delicate situation. How to tell him that it had already been done? Fortunately – thanks to his extreme good manners – the incident passed off smoothly without any embarrassment.

It was with a very light heart that I attended a cocktail party that evening in honour of French fashion, given by the most important English *couturiers*, the Top Ten.

My second glowing recollection of England is equally associated with Princess Margaret. This was in 1954 when she attended a showing of my clothes at Blenheim Palace, organized by the Duchess of Marlborough, in aid of the Red Cross. The Duchess had visited the avenue Montaigne several months previously to arrange the show, and we had admired the *chic* of her tall figure seen to great advantage in her elegant Red Cross uniform.

The thirteen mannequins who were chosen for the visit to Blenheim arrived the evening before the show, accompanied by Mme de Turckheim, and the *Service de la Presse*. Two of us preferred to go by boat – myself, and Renée with her famous horror of the air. The mannequins had supper at the palace, and were then boarded out at the houses of the Duchess's neighbours, or hotels in Woodstock.

When I arrived the next morning, my first thoughts were completely unrelated to fashion: I was struck dumb with admiration at the magnificence of Blenheim itself, the beauty of the park in which the leaves were now red, and the exquisite lake. The palace itself had been built for the Duke of Marlborough, by Queen Anne, in recognition of his great victories over the French. When I saw the two flags of France and England fluttering together in the afternoon wind over the palace, I silently asked Marlborough's pardon for having set up the triumphant standard of French fashion in such a place. At any moment I expected his indignant ghost to join the line of mannequins.

The poor girls, incidentally, had never felt so nervous in all their lives, as they paraded through fourteen *salons*, all hung with tapestries celebrating the defeat of the French. Used to the tiny showing space of the French *salons*, they found it difficult to adjust themselves to showing to two thousand people, through what seemed acres of rooms: they also had to remember to curtsy to the Princess as well.

This show at Blenheim, which is of course one of the rare showings of my models which I have actually attended, remains in my memory for several reasons, quite apart from the beauty of the setting. Just as it ended, I was assailed by a charming crowd of Red Cross nurses, dressed in uniform, like the Duchess, who pressed me and my mannequins for autographs. I was then made an honorary member of the English Red Cross, and presented with a diploma to that effect by Princess Margaret.

I learnt afterwards that for the girls, at least, all the excitement did not end with the end of the show. I myself, worn out, had taken the boat train back to Paris once the show was over, but the mannequins remained at Blenheim for a dinner and dance organized by the Duchess, and finally set out for London in the small hours of the morning. But in the general confusion of leaving Blenheim, and arriving in London so late, there was a muddle with the luggage. Everybody had everybody else's beauty box and over-night suitcase. As the models were distributed among half a dozen London hotels, it would have been the height of folly to drive madly in a taxi round the sleeping city to try and straighten the confusion out. Lia burst into a storm of tears and Mme de Turckheim was left trying in vain to rally the morale of her troupe, which had to depart at six o'clock the next morning – it was getting on for that already – in order to be ready to show at the avenue Montaigne in the afternoon.

All this time, my desire to have a house of my own actually set up in London was growing: it was in fact my good friends Simone and Serge Mireman who helped me to realize the project. The first show came fully up to my expectations and I was greatly moved by the excellent Press reception which it was given. Among the English journalists who attended it I should like to mention particularly Iris Ashley who knows how to write intelligently on a subject on which so much nonsense is often written. At Dior we always notice her absence or her presence, keenly, and wait eagerly to hear her impressions of our latest showing.

In spite of the founding of my own English house, I have one more tender memory of bringing my own collection to London when, in April 1955, Lord Inverclyde, chairman of the 'Friends of France', founded in Glasgow during the war to assist the French sailors from Brest evacuated there, and the honorary secretary, Mr E. J. Vacher, decided to give a soirée to help raise funds, and asked me to bring over my mannequins. There were actually two shows – one at the Central Hotel, Glasgow, and one at Gleneagles, both in the presence of a brilliant company. Present were M. Chauvel, the new Ambassador of France and his wife, the Lord Provost and his wife, and all the Scottish nobility, among them the delightful Duchess of Buccleuch. Embarrassed by such a wealth of celebrities, the announcer began to announce us with rather a rich preamble:

'My Lord Provost, Your Excellencies, your grace, my lords, ladies and gentlemen ...'

After the show, there was an unexpected contrast which delighted my French eyes: the parade of the girls in their delicate evening dresses was succeeded by Scottish reels danced by magnificent Scottish gentlemen in their kilts. It looked wonderful, but beneath the frenzied stampings of the dancers, the floor shook and bounced, and we were all nervous that it would collapse. Noticing the worried expressions on our faces, the Lord Provost told us that the wooden floor was specially constructed to shake beneath our feet, in order to give the reels added animation.

I lingered a little in Scotland. I had heard so much about its beauty that I had feared to be disappointed – on the contrary, I was even more struck by the beauty of the country, the castles, and the moors, than I had expected.

PART FOUR

THE ADVENTURE OF MY LIFE

— 17 —

MY EARLY YEARS

I have described the house of Christian Dior, and now I must bring myself, however reluctantly, to describe that other Christian Dior, in short, myself. Self-portrayal is always difficult. I wonder if one ever really knows oneself? Probably the simplest way to give an idea of my own character is to take you with me into various different houses where I have lived from childhood onwards. Possibly I am merely giving in to an avowed taste for interior decoration and architecture – my first vocation – but I am sure that this attempt at indirect biography will be more revealing than a straightforward account of my life.

Our house at Granville, like all Anglo-Norman buildings at the end of the last century, was perfectly hideous. All the same I look back on it with tenderness as well as amazement. In a certain sense, my whole way of life was influenced by its architecture and environment.

My parents bought it as a young married couple, a year or two after I was born. It stood on top of a cliff – which was later completely built over – and in the midst of a fair-sized park, whose young trees grew up, as I did, against the wind and the tides. This is no figure of speech, since the park hung right over the sea, which could be seen through the railings, and lay exposed to all the turbulence of the weather, as if in prophecy of the troubles of my own life.

To my child's eyes a pinewood fifty yards long meant a virgin forest. It has not lost this meaning for me, for today I should be overpowered by its high branches. But the walls which encompassed the garden were not enough, any more than the precautions encompassing my childhood were enough, to shield us from storms.

This house was at Granville, in the Manche, where my father owned factories for making fertilizers and chemicals, founded in 1832 by a great-great-grandfather who had been one of the first men to have the idea of importing guano from Chile into Europe. All the family was of Norman blood, except for the drop of '*douceur angevine*' brought in by my mother, the only thin person with a small appetite in our clan of good livers and hearty eaters. Granville itself, from which we were separated by half a mile, was for nine months of the year a peaceful little port and for the three summer months an elegant suburb of Paris. In those days all the facilities for travel which have lately turned summer visitors into nomads and bathing places into camping-sites did not yet exist. Granville, like all the smart Norman seaside places, had a regular influx of faithful clients. Dancing-classes for the young, the casino with its *petits chevaux* and light music, and flower-festivals, all were sure to be crowded by a Parisian public that had come to the seaside with its trunks, children, and servants, and was determined to preserve its own way of life unscathed.

For the other nine months, as we were cut off in our property like an island, far from the commercial atmosphere of the town, we saw hardly anybody. This isolation suited my tastes. A passion for flowers inherited from my mother meant that I was at my happiest among plants and flower-beds. My predilection influenced even my reading and, apart from those few books which made their mark on my whole childhood, my chief delight was to learn by heart the names and descriptions of flowers in the coloured catalogues of the firm of Vilmorin and Andrieu.

From the bedside books I had as a child, I remember above all Perrault's *Contes* with the Gustave Doré illustrations, and a very 'modern' story with pictures by Metivet. I was thrilled by these pictures, as I was to be thrilled later by the decor of the great room of the *Nautilus* in *Twenty Thousand Leagues Under the Sea*, which has remained for me the pinnacle of luxury and beauty. My early years were those of a very good, very well-brought-up little boy, watched over by vigilant *fräuleins*, and seemingly quite incapable of mingling in the hurly-burly of life.

At the beginning of this book I described my reluctance to leave my home for an instant – a reluctance which did not stop my first children's parties from making a great impression on me. I could be amused for hours by anything that was sparkling, elaborate, flowery, or frivolous. The Newfoundlanders returning or a three-master bringing back guano to store for the family business were real excitements indeed, but they interested me far less. As for the few visits I made to my father's factories, they have left appalling memories: I am sure my horror of machines and my firm resolve never to work in an office or anything like it date from then.

My childhood home was roughcast in a very soft pink, mixed with grey gravelling, and these two shades have remained my favourite colours in *couture*. As my mother had a passion for green plants, a protuberance had been stuck on to the front of the house without the least attempt at harmony – a 1900 wrought-iron con-servatory. Years later, when I moved to Paris, my first care was to find a house with the same feature.

The front door opened on to an entrance hall and the begin-ning of a big flight of stairs. The whole of this area was decorated in imitation pitchpine picked out with bamboo borders. In the same way over the doors there was a kind of pagoda roof of bamboo and straw. Large panels painted in imitation of Japanese prints adorned the whole staircase. These versions of Utamaro and Hokusai made up my Sistine Chapel. I can remember gazing at them for hours on end, as, perched on some exotic foot-stool of poker-worked leather, I would timidly finger the rustling beads of a blind. How bruised I was when I uncoiled from one of these so-called seats, designed for everything except sitting on!

Those long meditations left me with a strong taste for the *Japonaiseries* one sees on screens. I still love those silks embroidered with flowers and fantastic birds and use them in my collections.

The drawing-room was done up in Louis Quinze in complete contrast to modernistic styles, and genuine and false were delight-fully mingled. Cabinets with the glass divided into sections by gilt, were for me an inexhaustible source of wonder. Behind the glass thronged marquises and shepherdesses, supposedly from Saxony, with skirts trimmed in roses and lace, multi-coloured Venetian glass, forever catching some new ray of light, bonbon-dishes of every kind, and finally, enormous fans! Into the vases on the chimney-piece were crammed gymnemium (those 'feather-dusters' that I still love) and honesty.

The sitting-room was cosier and decorated in a Second-Empire style inherited from some grandparent; the walls were hung with a yellow moiré paper that I had the luck to find again for my house in Paris. As for my father's office, it filled me with a religious awe. It harboured a Renaissance wall-clock – pewter adorned with halberdiers that seemed terribly formidable to me and a mask of a Negress that looked as if she was about to eat you. Musketeers engraved after Roybet, blustering and mustachioed, completed my trepidation. Gentle though my father was, I never went into this room without a slight tremor of fear, either to be given a scolding or to wonder at the mysteries of the telephone, a thrilling novelty which had not yet palled.

I was frightened a little, too, by the dining-room – Henri Deux with its red and yellow stained-glass windows – although in the end I came to love it. To begin with, it was the dining-room, and I was already rather greedy; and then it was done up in the style of the *Contes* of Perrault that I loved so much. Lions and mythical creatures reared up at random on sideboards and cupboards, and a very pretty lady in Renaissance garb smiled down from a window-pane. My delight could not resist the assaults of time; today, by reaction, I am unfairly prejudiced against the furnishings of the *châteaux* of the Loire, and only by dint of great will-power have I come to appreciate the most beautiful Renaissance furniture.

In my own room I was particularly fond of the round plaque in the middle of the ceiling from which hung a night-light of multi-coloured glass, casting gleams that transformed my convalescence from measles and chicken-pox. Nearby was the play-room, with a dark cupboard into which my brother went more often than I. But the place I loved more than any other – was this fate? – was the linen-room. There the housemaids and seamstresses, hired for the day, told me fairy stories of devils and sang *Hirondelle du fau-*

bourg or the cradle-song from *Jocelyn*. Dusk drew on, night fell and there I lingered, forgetting my books and my brother, absorbed in watching the women round the oil-lamp plying their needles. This, then, was the happy and enticing life in the country from which my parents suddenly snatched me by deciding to live in Paris. From that time I have kept a nostalgia for stormy nights, fog-horns, the tolling of the cemetery-bell, and even the Norman drizzle in which my childhood passed.

Every year we used to pay a visit to our grandparents in Paris, a visit of which I have fairy-tale memories. It meant for me the discovery of electricity and the discovery of three books, *Michel Strogo*, *Les Pilules du Diable*, and *Round the World in Eighty Days* – and also of the cinematograph then showing at Dufayel's.

I was five years old, a wonderful age to see and retain every impression before the arrival of the depressing logic of the 'age of reason'. I thank heaven I lived in Paris in the last years of the *Belle Époque*. They marked me for life. My mind retains the picture of a time full of happiness, exuberance, and peace, in which everything was directed towards the art of living. The general care-free atmosphere derived from the illusion that the existence and capital of the rich as well as the thrifty lives of the poor were immune from any sudden reverse. The future, it seemed, could only hold greater comfort for everybody.

To reach the metropolis, a nightmare journey was necessary in one of the first Peugeot limousines, which were truly gigantic, not only to my childish eyes. This machine included four rows of benches and folding seats, on which we took nine places – four children, my parents, my grandmother, the governess, a house-maid, and a man we called then the 'handyman'. All of us were shrouded in dust-protectors, our faces swathed in veils, the women topped with cumbersome feathered hats, and the young boys with dashing *Jean-Barts*. Over our heads the heavy pile of luggage and spare tyres filled up the copper rack on the roof. What rapture, after innumerable strikes and punctures, to arrive at last at La Muette, rue Richard Wagner (how silly to change it to rue Albéric-Magnard, after the outbreak of war!)

Our new house, breaking with the *Japonaiseries* of Granville – a legacy of the Universal Exhibition – showed its modernism by a resolute eighteenth-century style. It was there that I discovered and was conquered for ever by 'Louis Seize-Passy' with its white-enamelling, doors with little bevel-edged panels, many window-flounces, macramé net curtains, panels of cretonne or damask depending on the degree of luxury of the room, interspaced with rococo flowers thought to be 'Pompadour' but which were in fact already 'Vuillard'. Nothing could be more welcoming, more warm, and at the same time lighter than these houses lit by electric fittings shaped like tulips or Louis Seize candelabra in brackets, with flames moulded in ground-glass. Austerity of style or judgement had not yet wrought its havoc. From my bedroom window – we lived on the fourth floor – I could see, on one side, the trees of the park of La Muette (later to be the hôtel Henri de Rothschild) and, on the other, at the end of the street, a huge intoxicatingly Gothic house, which has now been pulled down.

Nearer at hand I was intrigued by a house of only one storey – I could not understand why – with a colonnaded loggia overhanging the too-narrow front door. Forty years later, I was able to penetrate the mystery, since that is actually the house in which I live today. But the supreme wonder stood not far away, in the rue Octave-Feuillet, a real Persian minaret of 1910, with a roof glazed blue and gold, which the ridiculous severity of urban theory caused to be destroyed. What a pity! It was the solitary substantial reminder of the 'Persian' fashion brought to Paris in the train of the Ballets Russes. The Iribe style reigned everywhere. Nobody talked of anything but Nijinsky, the Persian Ball given by the Marquise de Chabrillan, divided skirts, hobble-skirted dresses, and the tango. Louis Seize retreated, or died smothered in the cushions of Scheherazade.

1914 began with the famous eclipse and with ominous scandals; the Bonnot crew in the red motor-car started the fashion for gangsters. In secret I began to read Fantomas and Arsène Lupin. A well-behaved pupil of Gerson, I hardly received any black marks in spite of the annoyance I caused some professors by my habit of covering my school-books with innumerable outlines of a woman's leg in a high-heeled shoe.

The outbreak of war caught us by surprise at Granville, on holiday. At first our *fräulein* refused to go, since she thought, as everyone did, that the cataclysm was impossible. She lived completely as one of the family, but when war broke out, she declared to our terrified amazement that she was ready, if needs be, to go 'bang-bang' at the French soldiers. We were too young for wartime to be for us the period of *Le Diable au Corps*, but it was one of great freedom, and freakish lessons under the guidance of teachers who were more or less freaks themselves.

During this time the womenfolk, kept busy with making bandages, working in hospitals, getting letters from the front, and having therapeutic sessions with their beloved wounded, left us alone. They were suddenly staggered by the arrival of a fashion magazine from Paris, announcing that the Parisiennes were wearing short skirts and 'flying-boots' with uppers of black, tartan, or bronze and laced up to the knees. Disapproval was unanimous and powerful. All the same, on that very day, each one hastened to order boots and short skirts from Paris by the evening post. Such was the heedless frivolity of an epoch which had to live through a conflict from which practically no one returned. A little later, despite the arrival of Big Bertha's shells on Paris, everyone was busy learning the first bars of *Tipperary* or the Y.M.C.A. songs. Hell reigned at Verdun, but in the rear all ears were alive to the rhythms of two-steps, and later to one-steps and fox-trots. But all this was only outward show; it was really a way of keeping up morale during the hardest ordeal men and women had ever had to undergo.

I will pass over the numerous changes of home and school caused by these events, and leap on to 1919, and our new and more lasting home in Paris. It was near the avenue Henri-Martin, in a flat where yet another eighteenth-century style reigned; it was thought to be very pure, but was in fact only eighteenth-century à la 1920.

This was the post-war period, a completely new epoch and a fresh start for everyone, including us fifteen-year-olds. We were wonderfully in keeping with our times. Officially I was supposed to be preparing my *bachot* for the Tannenberg course, but already, with my friends, I was falling under the influence of music, literature, painting, and all the manifestations of the new trend in the arts. One had to follow the crowd by not missing a private view, or a surprise-party, and by sharing with the century itself the unique privilege of belonging to the age of folly; there were nights without sleep and Negro music, blinds without hangovers, light amours, and serious friendships. I explored the four corners of the new Paris, alive with inventions, cosmopolitan, intelligent, prodigal with truly novel novelties. I used to frequent the picture-shops in the rue de la Boétie and, soon, certain more select galleries on the Left Bank, like the tiny stall of Jeanne Bucher, the austere and charming priestess of the Primitives and the Cubists. Modern art still had something of the Black Mass about it. Besides, black was in vogue. The influence of the war – mourning and black-out – combined with cubist severity, had banished from houses jade and gold cushions, and violet and orange blinds, in short the whole orgy of oriental colours, the short-lived conquerors of 1910 Louis Seize white.

No doubt the Dunand lacquers, Rhulmann macassar consoles, and Coromandel screens retained their sumptuous sway in grand hotels, dance-floors, and the rooms of showy artistes like Spinelly or Fernande Cabanel. But the unconditional revolution of Le Corbusier and Pierre Charreau was carried out with the clean sweep of a Saint-Just or of a Robespierre and banished all ornamentation. Everything had to be functional, whether architecture, furniture, or clothing. And, as the decade from 1920 to 1930 was a rich one, luxury was shown in subdued materials – reinforced cement, plain wood. In fashion Chanel ordained jerseys and tweeds; Reboux, cloche hats in bare felt without any trimmings. By contrast with the rationalism of the applied arts, the Fine Arts, painting, poetry, and music became inconsequential. Bonnard, Vuillard, Ravel, and Debussy, all seemed too indistinct, and a little out of fashion; the new gods were Matisse, Picasso, Braque, Stravinsky, and Schönberg. The Dadaists freed language from the tyranny of precise meaning. And dominating every *avant-garde* effort, the beacon of Jean Cocteau illuminated and revealed all.

The bar called the 'Bœuf-sur-le-Toit' was the Lhasa of this gay esotericism. It seems odd that in 1956 people tax with *avant-garde* ideas and futuristic tastes the self-same works and masters that we were admiring between the ages of fifteen and twenty and who, for ten years, had already been famous among our more enlightened elders, led by Guillaume Apollinaire.

With so many things to distract me, I cannot think how I succeeded in passing both my *baccalauréats*. The time had come to turn from a school-boy into a student. Driven by my love of architecture, I suggested to my family that I should study the Fine Arts. There was an outcry! I was not allowed to join the Bohemians. To gain time and to enjoy the greatest possible liberty, I was enrolled as a student of Political Science in the rue Saint-Guillaume, which entailed no commitments. Such was the hypocritical way in which I contrived to carry on the life I liked.

What a hectic life! German expressionistic films with Conrad Veidt and Louise Brooks, the Ballets Russes replacing Bakst and Benoit with the new Cubist designers, and the Swedish ballets – so *'avant-garde'* with their scandalous shows. Cocteau's *Les Maries de la Tour Eiffel* set to music by Six and with Jean and Valentine Hugo's decor, and *Entr'acte* by René Clair, and Satie. And on the stage Giraudoux, Claudel, or Chekhov.

Think of Bruckner's *Le Mal de la Jeunesse*, forerunner of Existentialism, performed in rooms which were sometimes only outhouses. Then we discovered the archaic; the art of the Negroes, of China, and Peru ... nothing was too primitive for us! In the circus there were the Fratellini, on the music-hall Mistinguett, Chevalier, the Dolly sisters, and, soon after, Josephine Baker. Songs came from Damia, the uncontested queen of realism, from Raquel Meller who bombarded the room with violets, from Fortuné, and from Bourvil and Trenet. On her trapeze Barbette achieved the synthesis of man, woman, and bird of paradise. It was indeed at this time that everything which now seems the height of novelty to so many ill-informed people was painted, spoken, or done.

My parents were in despair at having a son who was so incapable of concerning himself with anything serious. They were wrong because, in this varied climate, I not only formed the taste, but also the firm bonds of friendship, which have formed, and always will form, the basis of my life.

— 18 —

FRIENDSHIPS AND FRUSTRATIONS

If I was asked, 'How did you get to know your friends?' I would answer that as we came from different backgrounds we met purely by chance, or rather in obedience to those mysterious laws christened by Goethe with the name of elective affinities. Would I say we had a family resemblance? It might be supposed so from the fact that some among us have stamped the art of their epoch with their personality. To tell the truth, however, we never dreamed of becoming one of those groups with a social theory like the Pleiade, the Encyclopaedists, the Barbizon School, or the Bateau Lavoir. We were just a simple gathering of painters, writers, musicians, and designers, under the aegis of Jean Cocteau and Max Jacob.

After my resignation from the *Sciences Po* (the course in political science) I had contrived, not without difficulty, to get my parents' permission to study musical composition. Very soon I was a passionate champion of the movement which had begun under the impulse of Satie and Stravinsky with the Groupe des Six, and then the Arcueil School. Curious evening parties were held in our home. Sitting on the floor, in the regulation semi-darkness of that date, we would play modern music of a kind that sent our elders into fits of horror. On those nights, my father and mother used to take fright and fly for sanctuary to their own rooms.

A young Dutch musician, who has since become a diplomat, brought Henri Sauguet to one of these sessions. His lively gaze, sparkling with cunning behind his spectacles, the immense mobility of his face, the intelligence and humour of his talk, in fact all the qualities of Latin alertness in this man from Coutras in the Gironde quite dazzled me. To me he seemed tremendously famous.

Had there not just been a concert at the Théâtre des Champs-Élysées itself where his works had been applauded? That night he played his *Françaises* on the piano and his music united us all. It was what I should have dreamed of writing if heaven had granted me the gift of true musicianship. Henri Sauguet appeared from his very first works as the reviver of the spontaneous, sensual, and anti-scholastic style. Soon we were fast friends and it was through him – one of the best composers of his generation – that I was to get to know the man who was to be one of the foremost painters of the time.

This was a fair young man, slender and smooth-cheeked, whose enormous blue eyes had already realized that the human face and people's lives were worthy of far greater attention and honour than the simplified still-lives of the Cubists or the geometrical figures of the Abstract painters. His name was Christian Bérard. His drawings taught one to transform daily life into a magic world of passion and nostalgia. I bought as many of his sketches as I could, and covered the walls of my room with his inspired paintings. Through Sauguet again, I came to know Pierre Gaxotte who took almost as much interest in music and dancing as in history, and Jean Ozenne, another friend, then in *couture*, who was to have a decisive influence on my as yet unforeseen career as a *couturier*. What extraordinary meetings those were, coloured by Montparnasse and Anglomania, where we ardently enjoyed the pleasures of friendship. Our bowler hats were the equivalent of today's high-necked jerseys – but we were inspired with the same burning curiosity as the youth of today.

Through successive postponements I had escaped military service, like all the students of my age. But, in 1927, the fireworks of the 1925 Exhibition had been set alight, and I had to join up. Naturally my family's stable and comfortable position had made me a professed anarchist, as well as a pacifist, and so l refused to train for the officers' squad. My time was passed as a sapper of the second class in the Fifth Genie de Versailles, a regiment which had the advantage of not taking me far from Paris. My new and austere life gave me time for contemplation and I meditated on the profession I should choose once I was free. I settled on the most sensible course, one that must have seemed the deepest folly to my parents, and became the director of an art gallery!

After I had turned a deaf ear to all their objections I was given some hundreds of thousands of francs, with the express condition that I was never to let my name appear in the title of the firm. To have one's name over a shop was considered by my parents to be the nadir of social shame. I went into partnership with a friend, Jacques Bonjean, to open a little gallery at the end of a rather squalid cul-de-sac off the rue de la Boétie. Our ambition was to have shows there centred on the masters we admired most: Picasso, Braque, Matisse, and Dufy, and the painters we knew personally and already held in high esteem; Christian Bérard, Salvador Dalí, Max Jacob, the Bergmann brothers. If only I could have been able to keep that stock of paintings which would now be of incalculable value, and which my family thought were worthless!

It was at an exhibition of the work of Max Jacob that I met a young poet, just arrived from the country, called Pierre Colle. He was soon to abandon poetry for picture-dealing. His flair, intelligence, and business sense brought him dazzling success, which was shattered all too soon by his untimely death. We quickly became intimate friends, for we both placed the same high value on friendship; indeed that year, 1928, really was a springtime of friendship, rich in blossom and with no clouds.

We often went to pay a call on our master and friend, Max Jacob. At that time he lived in the rue Nollet in a curious house, a sort of palace seen through the wrong end of a telescope. Comfortable rooms, moderate prices, and the pleasures of community life had enticed to the hôtel Nollet quite a cluster of young men of our own age, completely diverse in temperament and gifts, but united in their affection for Max, their horror of pedantry, and their worship of frivolity. In a wonderful atmosphere of *fous rires* and pranks, I came to know Maurice Sachs, devoured with desire to become a writer and already in spite of himself an adventurer, Georges Geffroy who was then a fashion-designer, Marcel Herrand, famous already, and André Fraigneau, a reader at Grasset's and not yet a novelist. Henri Sauguet lived two doors away, in the rue Truffaut. He used to come and work with Max Jacob on operettas that were never finished; on their covers Christian Bérard pencilled frontispieces and ideas for costumes.

What mad evenings they were! And what wonderful improvisations took place. To the music of a gramophone, Max, who seemed youngest of us all, would discard his slippers and dance in red stockings, mimicking a whole *corps de ballet* to Chopin's *Préludes*. Sauguet and Bérard, helped by lampshades, counterpanes, and curtains, would turn themselves into all the characters of history. It was my part in those first charades and those games with historical costumes at the hôtel Nollet that was to enable me, twenty years later, to act the '*Couturier* on tour' in Dallas, Texas, with the necessary gusto. That wonderful time when our youth ran free, the year 1928, a millennium in my eyes; everything and anything seemed likely to succeed. Our gallery had a not unpromising start, enough to reassure my family. After 1925 one could see the virus of speculation penetrating into those social strata which were traditionally best defended against the hideous lust for lucre. Everything had to make money; business and art as much as finance. Since youth is rebellious, I used to have frequent arguments with my father which ended with a slam of the door and the formidable expletive 'Dirty bourgeois!' which left the author of my days in dumbfounded consternation.

1929. The American slump, the forerunner of the imminent world crisis, passed almost unnoticed in Paris. America was still a distant country in those days. I heard friends talking about the embarrassment of some *couturiers* faced with the sudden disappearance of their New-World *clientèle* but I was as yet far away from this trade and, as for the stocks that slumped, no one doubted that they would soon be rising again.

1930. At the end of the holidays came a portent which alarmed me more than the bank crash. In our empty house, a mirror came unhooked by itself and smashed on the floor in a thousand smithereens. Misfortune came into our hitherto happy and sheltered family immediately. My brother was struck down with an incurable nervous disease, and my mother, whom I adored, suddenly faded away and died of grief.

Looking back on it now I see that it was fortunate that her death came when it did, although it marked me for life. My mother left us before she knew of the perilous future unfolding before us. For at the beginning of 1931 my father, who had put his capital into real estate, saw ruin come upon him in a few days. Everything that is now a secure investment: land, *objets d'art,* pictures – not to mention stocks and shares – had to be hurriedly sold out at the lowest price.

Ruin was complete. For my part these accumulating dramas resulted in a 'flight to the East'. The desperate search for a new solution for the problems that this crisis of capitalism had rendered acute drove me, very naïvely, to get together a few thousand francs and join a group of architects who were leaving for a course of study in the U.S.S.R.

I do not know what Russia looks like now that she is under Khrushchev, but I hope with all my heart that she appears sunnier and more smiling than she did on our arrival in Leningrad. The way in which we were interrogated and our passports seized from us, the look of the carriages crossing the square, and the faces and clothes of the crowd swarming round our band of twenty students who suddenly seemed millionaires, all told of distress. It is unnecessary, I think, to narrate in detail a voyage undertaken and described by so many with better qualifications than mine. We toured round on severely planned itineraries, strictly conducted by very pleasant ladies from Intourist, and even by one sham American woman-tourist, so obviously a spy that we were soon relieved of her company. Our guardian angels found it very difficult to keep us together and prevent us from seeing the hideous poverty then reigning everywhere. The facades of the palaces were crumbling; in the traffic-less streets, an empty-faced crowd patrolled before shops with empty windows. Foreigners were parked in hotels that had been luxurious before 1914, but now nothing in them worked. Food fit for a wartime siege did little to appease our appetites, sharpened by walking. If I had

not been attacked by bedbugs I might have sampled the monot-
onous poetry of the shores of the Volga. Only the Caucasus, the
fringe of the Black Sea – the Russian Riviera – seemed to me to
be pleasant and habitable, thanks to the climate.

In short, this journey to the U.S.S.R. in 1931 abounded with
surprises; I wondered at the country's civilization in times past, I
was disappointed by the horrible present, and admired this people's capacity to exist at such a low level of life without losing faith
in its future and its mission. To be fair, one must allow for the role
of the eternal East in this picture of poverty and disorder. Yet
nothing will make me alter my impression that under the Tsars
Russia knew a better way of life than the one I saw. It may be – I
hope so – that such a huge sacrifice will not have been accepted
and borne in vain. But I must say we breathed a sigh of relief when
our passports had been given back and the boat sailed out of Soviet
waters. We were glad to be going back to the West, even though
it was in the midst of a crisis, and for me, furthermore, the return
was clouded with deepest sorrows and cares.

The third-class cabins in our cargo boat serving the Black Sea
ports seemed to me luxury indeed. As for the bazaars of Trebizond,
stuffed with worthless trinkets, I thought on entering them I was
going into Ali Baba's magic cave. Our route surpassed itself in
beauty; and I saw for the first time Constantinople and Athens.
As the end of the voyage drew near I felt I should have to face new
trials. I did not know that as soon as I had landed in France I should
have to prepare for another journey, the one Céline would call by
a name so fitting to my new fate: *Journey to the End of the Night*.

In Marseilles a telegram awaited me. My partner told me that
he was ruined in his turn. I wondered what would happen and
what I should do. My family had gone back to Normandy since
they could no longer afford their flat in Paris. I was alone. For the
first time I felt I understood what life was about.

I left the house which had always been home, and since I could
not afford hotels, sought refuge in other people's houses. They
were always kind and welcoming. I hope that as I tried to keep as
quiet and self-effacing as possible I was not too much of a burden

to the friends who gave me their hospitality, never guessing that I would come back at night supperless.

I was busy trying to sell the pictures in the gallery, an incredibly difficult task in those panic-stricken times. Paintings which today would be worth millions of francs hardly fetched a few tens of thousands. With the rare exception of wealthy *patrons* and collectors like the Vicomte and Vicomtesse de Noailles and David Weill, dealers were forced to sell the pictures among themselves at ever-decreasing prices. The day one did not suffer a staggering loss one thought one had made a good deal. I separated from Jacques Bonjean, my partner, only to share in the even worse affairs of Pierre Colle. So we went on from losses to goods seized in exchange, all the while organizing surrealist abstract exhibitions by which we chased away the last private collectors.

The general crisis worsened; I had to start coming to the help of my family whose funds were growing ever less, and the situation seemed hopeless not only in my eyes, but in those of a whole generation. Today I consider that because misfortune was shared among several friends of the same age and of the same tastes our distress was less unbearable than it might have been. Countless times, tired of waiting in my shop for the unlikely arrival of clients, I took refuge for hours with Marcel Herrand at the hôtel Rochambeau, which, like the hôtel Voutillemont in the rue Boissy d'Angais managed by the charming Mlle Donne, had inexhaustible credit. This was essential, because some of us had decided, whatever happened, never to pay for anything. Maurice Sachs, the richest and most ruined of us all, formulated this new rule of life in the land of Despair.

In the end our deserted gallery closed its windows and doors. As we had to eat and drink sometimes, good Moyses, who ran the Bœuf-sur-le-Toit often welcomed us in the evening, as 'old clients' whom he had known in our better days. But his establishment, which had also been hit by the slump, had withdrawn from the rue Boissy d'Angais into a house that was due for demolition in the rue de la Penthièvre. Although he had lowered the prices, Moyses had been able to keep the glory of our dear 'Bœuf', and the rich clients who kept it going had no idea that this cosmopolitan centre was also a shelter for vagabonds.

I landed up sharing with my friend Bongard (who welcomed me later on the road to New York) two wretched attics where he was already living with one of his mistresses. Everything went; the roof, the water, the electricity, and later on money; the house which had in more glorious days given shelter to Franklin was doomed to the picks of the demolition-men. But nothing stops youth from laughing and having a good time. Those who were less badly off, and had some small means, hastened to rally us. For a night, with the help of a few bottles, a piano, and a gramophone we would keep away the mice as we invented fantastic amusements. Charades in fancy dress were raised to the dignity of an institution, and I can see us still, Bongard, his friends, and myself, dressed up as God knows what, trotting from carriage-door to carriage-door, to arrive on foot without being noticed at some masked ball. But we were dancing on a volcano that was just about to erupt.

After so many worries, and so many missed meals, the inevitable happened: I fell ill – seriously ill. I had to leave for a mountain climate at once. As there was no form of social insurance, my friends clubbed together to help me. Thanks to their generosity, I was able to spend a year, first at Font-Romeu, and then in the Balearic Islands, where the cost of living was a great deal lower than in France. It was during this retreat from Paris, where I had always been content to admire the artistic achievements of others, that I discovered in myself the desire to create something of my own. I learnt the art of tapestry making, and became tremendously enthusiastic about it. I then drew some designs for tapestry, and later considered setting up a workshop. I was discouraged both by my own lack of means, and by the general lack of interest in tapestry on the part of the public. Nevertheless I look back on this attempt to give vent to my artistic feelings with pride.

On my return to Paris, I found my family in desperate straits, having sold their last possessions of any value. I persuaded them to sell their remaining shares, and go and live in the South of

France; I then looked round for a regular job for myself. It was not without reluctance that I resigned myself to making the rounds of the various places which might offer employment – insurance companies, banks, accountants. It was scarcely the right moment to be seeking a job. I learnt to appreciate all the minor anxieties of the unemployed – the fear that I would not get to the newspaper kiosk in time to scrutinize the small ads, the hasty scanning in order to memorize the hopeful addresses, the rush to try and arrive ahead of the queue of other applicants. In the course of one of these sterile expeditions, I went and saw Lucien Lelong, in order to apply for some sort of office job. I shall never know quite what prompted me, but I suddenly heard myself blurting out the words:

'I think I would be more useful working on the actual *couture* side of the business.'

That remark marked the end of my downward progress. I was lucky enough to sell to the C.P.D.E. a large Dufy which I still had – a plan of Paris. Poiret had commissioned it in order to decorate his *Amours, Délices, et Orgues* at the fabulous time of the *Arts Décoratifs* Exhibition of 1925; several years later he was ruined, and sold it to me. This windfall gave me time to breathe, and allowed me to interrupt my vain pilgrimage round the Paris offices: I could also help my family. Jean Ozenne suggested that I should come and live with him, in his charming flat on the Quai Henri Quatre, which has a most beautiful view of the Seine, the square end of the Île Saint-Louis, and the distant Panthéon. There was nothing to indicate that Jean Ozenne would have an extremely successful theatrical career after 1945 – he was then a fashion-designer. Numbers of *couturiers* bought designs from him. Seeing that he was at work, and seeing that I was totally out of work, I set out to imitate him.

Not only did Jean encourage me and allow me to learn from his experience but he also suggested showing my designs to his regular clients at the same time as his own. An American friend of mine called Max Kenna, another designer, taught me to use the paint-brush, and how to mix my colours. Feeling very daring, I started to submit sketches to all the magazines. One evening, Jean returned in triumph: he had sold some designs of mine for 120 francs (at 20 francs each). It was the first money I had ever earned by my own creative inspiration. I was transported with joy. Those 120 francs, won for me by a faithful friend, were the first gleams of sun after a long night; they decided my future then, and they were to illuminate my whole life for the future.

It was in this fashion that I discovered my true *métier* – at the age of thirty. I went down to the South, in order to look after my family's affairs, and also to work hard at designing. It seems incredible to think that, despite my love of art, and my many artistic friends, I scarcely knew how to wield a pencil. For two months I worked night and day at producing ideas, and I finally went back to Paris, my pockets stuffed with designs, determined to win a place for myself in the world of fashion. My hat designs found plenty of buyers, but my dresses, which were decidedly less skilful, were correspondingly less successful. Two good friends of mine, Michel Brunhoff and Georges Geffroy, did not spare me their criticisms, and I was stung to further efforts. Living from hand to mouth on the proceeds of the few sketches I sold one by one at the price of interminable waits in waiting-rooms and offices, I laboured on. But this pilgrimage towards the establishment of my reputation, which lasted for two years, was infinitely less painful than the struggle for uncongenial employment which had preceded it: after all, I was fighting on a much more attractive battlefield.

I lived in the hôtel de Bourgonne, in the place de Palais-Bourbon, where the *clientèle* was divided between intellectuals of the pre-Sartre era – who were later to compose the fauna of the Café Flore – and provincials, attracted by the neighbourhood of Sainte-Clothilde, and their relations in the faubourg Saint-Germain. Georges Geffroy, who also lived there, introduced me to Robert Piguet who asked me to have several of my dresses made for his coming collection. At last I was able to see one of my designs put into practice! 1937 marked the end of my years of apprenticeship. I was no longer a humble designer who hung about waiting-rooms, but a designer whose name was known, and who made proper appointments for his visits. Most important of all,

I was doing well enough to realize the chief ambition of my life – and have a home of my own.

It was then comparatively easy to find a flat. It was while I was selling some designs in the rue Royale, that I saw the notice 'to let' at No. 10. I was shown five large rooms which had been empty for more than a year, and was told that I could have the floor above if I so wished. I settled for a rent of 8,000 francs a year, and found myself installed with my furniture, my bed, my pictures, and my few ornaments.

Admittedly the rooms were still very bare, but what did it matter? I had my home.

In 1938 Piguet moved to the Rond-point des Champs-Élysées, and asked me to go and work for him as a house designer. I was thrilled at the offer and instantly accepted. At last I would get to know the mysterious means by which an idea is transformed into a dress; I would make a shy, but fascinated, entrance into the universe of *premières* and workrooms; I would discover the secrets of cutting and stitching. Piguet was a charming but changeable master. His love of intrigue – which alone could awaken a flicker of gaiety in his cynical eyes – made it somewhat difficult to work for him. But he appreciated my ideas and the models I designed for him were genuinely successful. I shall always remember my beloved Christian Bérard introducing me to Marie-Louise Bousquet, as the creator of 'Café Anglais'. This was a dress of *pied de poule*, with a trimming of lace, inspired by Petites Filles Modèles, which had created a great stir that season. It was then that Marie-Louise Bousquet introduced me to Carmel Snow of *Harper's Bazaar*, and I really began to think that I had arrived.

What had in fact arrived even more surely than I had, was the fatal year of 1939. It made its appearance in a burst of follies, which always seem to precede a catastrophe. Paris had rarely seemed more scintillating. We flitted from ball to ball, under the surrealist presidency of Mme Schiaparelli. Fearing the inevitable cataclysm, we were determined to go down in a burst of splendour.

War finally came. I was mobilized at Mehun-sur-Yevre, the country of Agnès Sorel, and was rudely torn from my atmosphere of chiffon, and *paillettes*. I spent a year there, in sabots, with peasants from Berry. I quickly forgot *couture* in that very different atmosphere, for I was once more penniless, having saved nothing from my pre-war earnings. I found myself living for the first time in the depths of the country. I became passionately fond of it and developed a feeling for hard labour on the land, the cycle of the seasons, and the perpetually renewed mystery of germination. The *débâcle* of June 1940 left me, thank God, in the southern zone of France, where it was easy enough for me to join my father and sister at their retreat at Callian, a little village in the Var.

My experiences at Mehun had taught me that I had a strong streak of the peasant, so with my sister I decided to cultivate the little piece of land which surrounded the house. Callian has admirable soil for growing vegetables, and they fetched excellent prices on the market during this period of general restrictions. We pulled up flowers and rosebushes, and concentrated on runner beans and peas. In order to get through the three months which separated us from our harvest we lived off the 800 francs which I had been given on demobilization.

Then, a miracle, practically the last foreign money which can have been paid into France, reached me at Callian. A few weeks before the war, I had sent to America four or five pictures, all that remained of my defunct gallery, and which were unsaleable in Paris. Max Kenna undertook to sell them, and actually sent me a thousand dollars on the proceeds. Thus fortified, we awaited the harvest, which we intended to take to Cannes, or the neighbouring market, ourselves.

A good many Parisians had taken refuge in Cannes. I went there twice a week, and it was there I met Victor Grandpierre, and Marc Doelnitz, who organized theatricals at the big hotels to divert us. My time was not wholly occupied with my runner beans: I received news of *Figaro*, which had taken refuge at Lyons. Before the war, my friend Paul Caldagues had asked me to help with the woman's page of the paper, where my designs were appearing regularly. Now I was politely asked to send some sketches from my retreat; and I was delighted to take the opportunity of keeping my hand in.

When the inter-zonal communications became easier, we learnt that life in Paris was gradually resuming something approaching normality. The *couture* houses had re-opened their workshops, as much to provide employment for thousands of workers as out of patriotic pride, and Robert Piguet wrote asking me to take up my old job in his house. I hesitated a great deal. I disliked intensely the idea of returning to a humiliated and beaten Paris. And my new countrified mentality disliked the thought of the intrigues and labours of studio life. I also had to consider the future of our agricultural venture if it was left under the sole supervision of my sister. In short, it was not until the end of 1941 that I decided to accept Robert Piguet's offer.

When I eventually arrived back in Paris, I found Piguet extremely vexed at my tardy arrival. After beating about the bush for a bit, he confessed to me that weary of waiting for me, he had engaged in my place a young designer, previously at Chanel, called Antonio de Castillo. The fact that I heard his name for the first time in such unfavourable circumstances, has not prevented Castillo and me from becoming excellent friends. In any case, this temporary setback turned to my advantage, for Paul Caldagues, touched at my plight, introduced me to Lucien Lelong who engaged me there and then on the spot. The house of Lelong was an excellent *couture* school. There was a solid tradition of good workmanship, thanks to some remarkable *premières* directed by Nadine Cassandre. At Lelong, which was a much larger house than Piguet, I learnt a tremendous amount more about my new profession.

The creation of the models there was not my sole responsibility, for Pierre Balmain, who had worked at Lucien Lelong before the war, came and took up his old job. No malicious rivalry ever divided us during the years we worked together. Love of fashion took pride of place over love of self. Neither Balmain nor I will ever forget that Lelong taught us our profession, in spite of all the restrictions of wartime, and the constant fear of a sudden closing. Such an apparently frivolous and futile occupation risked earning the displeasure of the Germans: but somehow we managed to exist until the day of Liberation.

Lelong was actually in the midst of preparing his winter collection when we were liberated: several weeks later, to the amazement of the Allies, he was able to present them with a spectacle of living Parisian fashion.

I sometimes wonder how I managed to carry on at all during those years – for my sister, she with whom I had shared the cares and joys of the garden at Callian, had been arrested and then deported in June 1944. I exhausted myself in vain in trying to trace her. Work – exigent, all-absorbing work – was the only drug which enabled me to forget her. Fashion in those days was – well, I have already said enough about those hideous styles and monstrous hats at the beginning of this book. In the ten years since the war ended, I have had great pleasure in taking my revenge on those hideous styles.

— 19 —

PORTRAIT OF MYSELF

We all have our own little *faiblesse* which is at the same time a source of strength, because the thought of it whiles away the weary hours, and gives motive force to our toils. What is my particular weakness? I shall first of all reject those weaknesses which I do not share.

Unless there is something outstanding to be seen, I take little pleasure in entertainments like cinemas, cabarets, or nightclubs. I am sometimes asked why I so seldom design for the theatre, why my name so rarely appears on programmes. In my opinion, the art of the costumier is essentially different from that of the *couturier*. When Marcel Herrand asked me to design the costumes for Sheridan's *School for Scandal* in 1939, I was working anonymously at Piguet. These were the first costumes to which I put my name. Later I designed costumes for several films or ballets, but never with any particular pleasure. Designing for the theatre needs a quality of improvisation, of sacrifice of craftsmanship to the effect, which is alien to my temperament. I have horrifying memories of a ballet called *Thirteen Women* which I designed at the request of Boris Kochno and Christian Bérard. We ended by sewing the costumes on to the backs of the dancers, when they were already in position to dance across the stage.

If I dislike entertainments, I must confess that I am still less prone to reading. With the exception of Balzac, I never read novels; I am only really interested in books of history or archaeology. Painting of course was my first love, and in order to terminate the list of my favourite distractions, I will admit to a great weakness for cards. I spend hours bent over the Bridge or Canasta table, trying to penetrate its mysteries – a sign of intellectual poverty, perhaps, but it is best to be honest.

My *faiblesse*, as you will have guessed, is architecture, which has fascinated me ever since I was a child. Prevented by my family and by my circumstances from ever gratifying this passion, I found an outlet for it in *couture*. I think of my work as ephemeral architecture, dedicated to the beauty of the female body.

Couture has given me a further outlet for my passion, by providing me with the money to gratify it. With the money I received from my first collection, I was able to give rein to my natural inclination as a builder. At that time I was living in a country cottage near that of my friends Pierre and Carmen Colle, in the forest of Fontainebleau. It was there that I started to look for my country home. It was to be neither a *château*, nor a weekend villa, but a real rural retreat, a part of the countryside, preferably with a stream running through it.

This Rousseauesque dream found its expression near Milly, in the old mill of Coudret. Small, plain buildings, which had been stables, some barns, and the actual mill, surrounded a proper farmyard in the shape of a horse shoe. The ancient roofs were almost sound, and so were the lichen-covered walls, with the exception of one wing restored by the last owner in execrable taste. My first action was to hack off all his embellishments with an axe – to the consternation of the agent. I then turned my attention to making the house habitable in the style I wanted. The widely differing character of the rooms enabled me to decorate them all in the same *genre*, without fear of monotony. I wanted a house something like those houses in the provinces, those whitewashed convents with their well-polished parlours where children are brought to talk politely to their relations, of which I preserve tender memories. I wanted my first country home to look both lived in, and livable in.

My garden I entrusted to the care of the faithful Ivan, who had done wonders with my garden at Fleury: in spite of its size, I wanted it to look like the peasants' gardens which decorate the sides of the roads in my native Normandy. To achieve such an effect, the forest and the river had to be tamed, the weeds cleared away. Then I could retire into my bower of flowers, and listen in peace to the bells of Milly. I had constructed the hermitage of repose which my soul needed.

Scarcely was the mill finished than I was faced with the problem of a house in Paris, corresponding to the social demands of my official life. The flat in the rue Royale, which I had gradually furnished in a *fin de siècle* style to my taste, could not live up to my new responsibilities. I had to face the thought of leaving it and leaving, too, the four flights of stairs, which were no doubt holding in check the embonpoint that was the natural result of my love of good food!

I searched the whole of Paris, with the exception of Passy, which I sedulously avoided, true to the fashion of the moment, which dictated that one must at all costs live in the 7th Arrondissement. But it seemed that only Americans were capable of unearthing houses in the Guermantes district. I prospected in the avenue Hoche and Neuilly, but without success. Nothing seemed suitable. I won the reputation of being impossible to please at the house agents', until once more chance came to my aid.

One morning my principal agent telephoned me, and said in a weary voice:

'We've found a house which is for sale, but unfortunately it is in Passy, in the boulevard Jules-Sandeau!'

At that moment I experienced the famous sensation of '*temps retrouvé*': I rushed to the address I was given, and found to my delight that it brought me within fifty yards of rue Albéric-Magnard, the home of my youth. There was the balcony of columns, which had so fascinated me, in an exquisite little house which had been built in 1905 for an actress. Through the open door, I immediately felt that this was *my* house. It was true that it was laden with arabesques, festoons, and astragals, but the layout of the house was unexpected and delightful; it included a winter garden which immediately reminded me of Granville. Without more ado, without even consulting the architect, I took the house on the spot, and concentrated all my energies on the decoration of my new home.

The actress for whom the house had been built had lived a great deal in St Petersburg in the days of the Théâtre Marie, and became obsessed with fear of nihilists. Half blockhouse, and half love nest, the house was the exact opposite of what a peace-loving bachelor of 1950 needed. I commanded an army of decorators – Victor Grandpierre, Georges Geffroy, and Pierre Delbée from Jansen's – to make a proper town house for me, as urban as Milly had been rural.

It was to be filled with *objets d'art*, precious or worthless, so long as they appealed to my taste, and expressed my personality. A Matisse drawing was to hang side by side with a Gothic tapestry, a Renaissance bronze, a Jacob ornament. Good taste was much less important than my own taste, for after all, living in a house which does not suit you is like wearing someone else's clothes. I like an atmosphere which has been built up little by little out of the whims and fancies of the inhabitant. If I *had* to name my favourite style for a house, I would choose Louis Seize, but it would be 1956 Louis Seize, a contemporary and therefore sincere version.

As I finish this book, I am in the process of finishing the decoration of my house in Provence, at Montauroux, near Callian. I cannot describe this new house fully, since it is still not completed. It is simple, ancient, and dignified: I hope its dignity conveys the period of life which I am entering. I think of this house now as my real home, the home to which, God willing, I shall one day retire, the home where perhaps I will one day forget Christian Dior, *Couturier*, and become the neglected private individual again.

I am in fact at Montauroux as I write these last lines: fate has brought me into the calm and peace of the Provençal countryside to put the finish to my work. Night is falling and, with it, infinite peace. The avenue Montaigne seems far away, for I have spent the day among my vines, inspecting the future wine harvest. The first stars have come out, and are reflected in the pool opposite my window.

It is the moment to bring the two Christian Diors face to face, myself, and this Siamese twin of mine to whom I owe my success. It is fitting that we should meet here among the vines and the jasmine, for I am always more self-confident when I feel near to the soil.

What conclusions do I draw from this fateful meeting? First of all, he and I do not belong to the same world. He lives entirely in the century to which he owes his birth, he loves to revolutionize and to shock. I have never lost the simple tastes and habits of my Norman childhood, my love of solid, well-laid foundations.

It is for this reason that I have always tried to build my fashions on a solid base. True luxury needs good materials and good workmanship; it will never succeed unless its roots are profoundly embedded in sober influences and honest traditions. Lack of money is turning the present century away from frivolity: the modern *toilette* must be dependable and straightforward. Fantasy upon fantasy, extravagance upon extravagance, belong to the costumier, not the *couturier*. Fashion is destined to be worn elegantly in the streets and drawing-rooms, and must obey its own strict laws. Mlle Chanel gave the best definition of it when she said:

'*Couture* creates beautiful things which become ugly; while art creates ugly things which become beautiful.'

I would venture to correct Mlle Chanel in one respect: there is such a thing as the posthumous vengeance of fashion, and the ugly can become beautiful again with the passing of time. Nevertheless it is true that we work under an ephemeral star, and only precision of design, excellence of cut, and quality of workmanship can save us.

I believe that in my own fashion I have worked on the same principle as the other members of my circle of friends. Christian Bérard paints faces devoured by a burning passion in reaction to the laws of Cubism which forbade the reproduction of the human figure for twenty years. Francis Poulenc and Henri Sauguet have opposed lyrical music to pedantic composition. Pierre Gaxotte's heartfelt *Histoire des Français* contrasts with the Michelet school of history. Within my own sphere I have been equally reactionary; I have battled against everything that I have considered as triumphing for the wrong reason. I have tried to impose my taste and temperament upon my clothes, for a model must always take its public by storm. As a garment, it must respect certain laws: but as a *toilette*, it must dare certain extravagances. There is room for audacity in the traditions of *couture*.

A particular fashion pleases, or ceases to please, according to complex influences. The most successful fashion wears itself out the quickest, because it is over-imitated and over-propagated. There will always be certain women who cling to a particular style of dressing, because they wore it during the time of their greatest happiness, but white hair is the only excuse for this type of extravagance.

Finally, how shall I explain the miracle of fashion itself? The continued miracle of the popularity of *couture*, and the public interest displayed even in the lives of the humble *couturiers*. I believe that the answer lies in this very miraculous quality which fashion surely possesses: in the world today *haute couture* is one of the last repositories of the marvellous, and the *couturiers* the last possessors of the wand of Cinderella's Fairy Godmother. The need for display which is dormant in all of us, can express itself nowadays in fashion and nowhere else: that is why the papers devote yards of space to discussing fashion, and that is why the *couturiers* are still able to present a sumptuous new collection each season. The dresses of this collection may be worn by only a few of the thousands of women who read and dream about them; but high fashion need not be directly accessible to everyone: it is only necessary that it should exist in the world for its influence to be felt.

Fashion has its own moral code however frivolous: when someone objects to the fact that certain of my *toilettes* are ill-suited to the serious times in which we live, I reply that a period of happiness is no doubt on the way, when these frivolous fashions will come into their own. The maintenance of the tradition of fashion is in the nature of an act of faith. In a century which attempts to tear the heart out of every mystery, fashion guards its secret well, and is the best possible proof that there is still magic abroad.

I am speaking lightly of fashion – but my tone is tinged with respect. The great adventure which constitutes Parisian *couture* is not merely a Temple of Vanities: it is a charming outward manifestation of an ancient civilization, which intends to survive.

Suddenly I come to view my other self with genuine respect, perhaps the wretched *couturier* has something to be said for him after all. I view him with an altogether more friendly eye. His role is to be a guardian of the public taste – and that is a valuable role indeed. Meanwhile I can lurk in his brilliant shadow, and console myself that he has left me the best part of our dual personality – I can take care of the actual work, from the idea to the dress, while he maintains a dazzling worldly front for us both.

Ultimately, therefore, I accept the identification of myself with him, and ten years after the founding of my house, am content that we two, the great *couturier* and the shrinking nonentity, should bear the same name.

INDEX

Christian Dior is referred to as CD throughout.